HEADLINES AND DEADLINES

HEADLINES
AND DEADLINES

A MANUAL FOR COPY EDITORS

by ROBERT E. GARST

and THEODORE M. BERNSTEIN

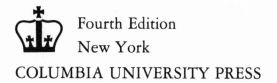

Fourth Edition
New York
COLUMBIA UNIVERSITY PRESS

Columbia University Press
New York   Guildford, Surrey

Library of Congress Cataloging in Publication Data

Garst, Robert Edward, 1900–
  Headlines and deadlines.

  Includes index.
  1. Copy-reading.   2. Newspapers—Headlines.
I. Bernstein, Theodore Menline, 1904–
II. Title.
PN4784.C75G3   1982   070.4'15   81-21690
ISBN 0-231-04816-5   AACR2
ISBN 0-231-04817-3 (pbk.)

p 10 9 8 7 6 5 4 3 2

CONTENTS

NOTE FROM THE PUBLISHER

PLANS FOR the fourth edition of this book had been initiated before the deaths of both Mr. Garst and Mr. Bernstein. Both authors had in fact submitted their revisions for the new edition, but unfortunately they did not live to participate in the editorial and production stages.

The publisher gratefully acknowledges the assistance of Mr. Garst's widow, Edith Evans Asbury, a reporter on *The New York Times* for twenty-nine years, in resolving editorial questions. Acknowledgment is also made to the late Richard T. Baker, professor of journalism at Columbia University, for his help in resolving questions of a similar nature.

A special note of thanks is due to James F. Lynch, for thirty-four years a copy editor at *The New York Times*, who took the photographs that appear in chapter 4, updated the organizational charts in chapter 1, and furnished valuable last-minute information on the current state of computer technology.

The greatest instance of editorial changes made without the authors' participation consisted in updating examples of newspaper practice. Some of the examples carried over from earlier editions no longer seemed appropriate. In selecting new examples, every effort was made to adhere to the principles educed by Mr. Garst and Mr. Bernstein, and to use substitutes as close as possible in style to the authors' original choices.

In one area—the use of the masculine pronoun—no change

was made from the authors' original practice. While recognizing the change in attitudes in recent years that has made such usage a sometimes prickly matter of contention, the publisher felt that imposing beliefs on the authors that had not been discussed with them would be more reprehensible than maintaining a practice that some readers might find distasteful.

FOREWORD

ANYONE WHO has studied or practiced American journalism recognizes the key role of the copy editor. It is these often unsung heroes (and, increasingly, heroines) who largely set the standards of lucid and readable prose in American newspapers, broadcasting and wire-service output. Most of us know of winners of Pulitzer Prizes, great reporters but not great writers, who would be also-rans if their prose had never been touched by a sympathetic, understanding and skilled copy editor.

As implied in "Electronic Editing," the wholly new chapter that the authors added to this edition, the impact of the able copy editor is increasing. This results from the simple mechanical fact that computerized equipment greatly facilitates the transposition of sentences and paragraphs, the inserting of clarifying words or clauses, and the general polishing of prose.

If copy editors are often heroes, Bob Garst and Ted Bernstein were the heroes' heroes. Probably no two persons played more of a role in raising the level of journalistic prose in this century. As teachers at the Graduate School of Journalism of Columbia University, the team affectionately known as "Garstein" had marked influence on more than a generation of rising young journalists. As authors, they have influenced many more. And, as key staff editors on *The New York Times*, both played significant roles in helping set the patterns that many other news organizations have followed. Garst, as the student of journalistic organization and practices, and Bernstein, as the urbane arbiter of effective English, made an ideal team.

It is a cause for rejoicing that these two gifted men completed their revisions for the fourth edition of *Headlines and Deadlines* before their recent deaths. The book embodies basic principles and practices that will have validity as long as journalism seeks to be honest, clear and reliable. In such matters as language and deft wordmanship, it is as up-to-date as these two masters, assisted by sophisticated young professionals, could make it.

As Dean of Columbia's Graduate School of Journalism for twelve years and as publisher of the Columbia Journalism Review, I considered this book a bible for the young editor. This latest updated edition should continue to play that role as a valued handbook both for copy editors and for journalists generally.

Edward W. Barrett

February 1982

PREFACE

COPY EDITING is one field in which the demand for workers usually exceeds the supply. This is likely to be permanently so because in an ideal sense there never will be a copy editor who knows enough to fill the requirements of the job thoroughly. The ideal copy editor not only would have a complete mastery over the technical work, such as the editing of copy and the writing of headlines, but would possess sound and swift judgment, would be an expert rhetorician and grammarian and would be thoroughly versed in government, politics, astrophysics, home gardening, shoes, ships, sealing wax and all subjects that find or are likely to find a place in the kaleidoscopic enterprise that is the modern newspaper.

Obviously, then, no book can furnish all the equipment that the copy editor is expected to bring to his work. A book cannot instill judgment; it cannot supply a broad mental background, which after all, is cumulative. But what it can do is to explain the technique of copy editing. That is the aim of the present volume.

What the authors have sought to do is to set before journalists—practicing, as well as aspiring—the best standards of the metropolitan press. This involves no reflection on rural journalism, for the two are not things apart; rural practice is, rather, an adaptation of metropolitan practice to the more personal and informal needs of the small-town newspaper.

While, from the point of view of the rural press, the standards presented may be too rigid, from the point of view of
the individual newspaperman they are indispensable if he
wishes to follow his profession into whatever field it may
beckon him. The journalist trained for rural practice alone
would be dismayed if suddenly he found himself on a city
daily. On the other hand, the journalist equipped with metropolitan standards could adapt himself almost immediately
to rural technical requirements.

Hence, what this book seeks to do is not to reform journalism, but to train journalists. Its purpose is to give so thorough and basic instruction that the copy editor will be able to
work on the desk of a newspaper anywhere.

The copy editor's work falls naturally into two main divisions: editing copy and writing headlines. This book is, therefore, similarly divided. Included in the section on editing is
a condensed list of "Abused Words" which calls attention to
the more common errors made in newspapers. Appended to
the section on headlines is a "Headline Vocabulary of Related
Words" in which the words are grouped by their meanings
under key words listed alphabetically. This list, which should
prove useful to the headline writer, is believed to be the first
of its kind so compiled.

The importance of the copy editor's function is treated elsewhere. Suffice it to set down here that the authors consider
it to be the backbone of the newspaper and, as such, deserving
of a book all its own. Editorial writers may, within their limited
confines, be brilliant and persuasive; reporters may be enter-
prising and thorough; but it is the copy editors who have in
their keeping ultimately the newspaper's reputation for accuracy, for attractiveness and for intelligence.

The authors acknowledge a debt to colleagues who have

given wise counsel on the contents of this book, but who, in the true newspaper tradition, are content to "keep their names out of print." The authors feel, however, that especial thanks are due to the late Professor Charles P. Cooper, of the Columbia School of Journalism, who suggested the book and guided and inspired its preparation.

Examples are largely taken from *The New York Times*.

R. E. G.
T. M. B.

New York

PART ONE COPY

1. NEWSPAPER ORGANIZATION

THE EMPHASIS in newspaper work has long—too long, perhaps—been put upon the reporter. While there is no wish to
take from the reporter credit for many superb contributions
to the excellence of the modern newspaper, it ought to be
realized that there is someone who stands between the reporter
and the critical public—the copy editor. The sparkling, swift,
entertaining story, signed by John Jones of *The Daily Star*,
draws comment and approbation, but it is not often recognized, even by his fellows, that the copy editor's share in the
creation of the gem may be as great as if not greater than that
of John Jones, reporter.

It is not seldom that the wit, ingenuity and craftsmanship
of the copy editor rescue from the limbo of unread newspaper
stories the uninspired work of John Jones. It is the editorial
eye as much as the reportorial keyboard that puts before the
public daily the readable information of the world's happenings. It is the copy editor who is essentially the guardian of
what gets into the newspaper and how it looks when it gets
there. The copy editor detects the errors, corrects the English,
cuts out the dead wood of verbiage, tones the story up to its
proper pitch or down to the level required by good taste or
the libel laws.

The appeal of the reporter's work is great; the activity, the
contact with the world, with its great men and with its ideas,
make the stimulation of the job unparalleled in any profession.

But the copy editor is closer to the heart of the newspaper's power; he is indeed, its heart. Under his eyes flow the accounts of all important happenings anywhere. This sense of closeness to vital things, plus the ability to shape information about them so that their importance will be shown in true perspective, make the copy desk job second to none.

Whatever the respective merits of the copy editor's and the reporter's work, both are cogs in a machine that has only one object: to gather and publish quickly information of events. The newspaper strives to put before its readers daily the interesting and important happenings that have occurred or have become known in the preceding 24 hours. Information, to be news, must be new, fresh, immediate, and it is the reporter's task to gather and write it quickly and the copy editor's to hasten it through the news machine into print.

To meet the requirements of his position properly, the copy editor must have a detailed knowledge of the highly developed organization that has been set up to speed copy to his desk and through his hands into print. The machine is linked to all parts of the world by radio, cable, telephone, telegraph, ship, plane, train, and satellite. Internally the newspaper office is equipped to transfer words from copy to print in minutes. The effort is perpetual to draw widespread information to a focal point and send it out again as a newspaper.

Not only is speed requisite in the gathering and the printing of the news; it is paramount also in imparting information to the reader. The newspaper story is constructed so that the most information can be told in the least time. To convey its message effectively, the story must be clear, concise, emphatic. The important facts must come first, the less important follow in their order. The headline, likewise, is a device to tell the news quickly. It is a further condensation of a story that has already been stripped to its essentials in the introduction. The headline must be specific and forceful. Excess must be shorn away; facts must be set forth to the point of baldness.

It must not be supposed that this speed is uncontrolled; it is that of efficient men trained to their work. It is not achieved at the expense of thoroughness or accuracy, without which their efforts would be valueless.

THE MANAGING EDITOR

At the head of the news organization is the managing editor. From him or through him comes the driving force that keeps the machine at its most efficient point. On him depends the morale of the organization.

His chief efforts are concerned with news gathering. He is informed of the world's events and, through subordinate editors, obtains accounts of these happenings for the newspaper's readers. Essentially his object is simple; actually the attainment of that object is extremely complex. His plans cannot be hit and miss; they must be laid with minute care. It is in this that the qualities of the managing editor are shown to the best advantage.

For example, let it be supposed that the newspaper prints a small story of an outbreak of hostilities in Peru. This item is read by the managing editor as a routine part of his duties. Has it possibilities? Is it worth while to send a special correspondent to watch the situation? A decision on this will depend very little on the facts given in the story. It will depend rather on his knowledge of the general conditions in Peru, whether these are such that there might be further disorders, what effect such violence might have on the country itself and what effect it might have on the relations of the United States with Peru and Peru's with other nations. Answers to such questions hinge not upon the immediate situation, but upon the managing editor's store of historical knowledge about the country and its problems. It hinges also on a sensing of possibilities, in short on news sense.

If he decides to send a correspondent, the next problem is to select the right person. The assignment is a delicate and a responsible one, perhaps even dangerous. The choice must be wise. In making it, the editor relies on knowledge of the staff's abilities and character. Success or failure in obtaining a story often depends on selecting the right person for the assignment.

The next step is getting the reporter to the scene, equipped with detailed instructions, if necessary, of what to do. This is often vital in order to maintain contact between the office and the reporter. How to send stories is frequently a major difficulty. There may be a censorship, or for other reasons communication may be erratic. Various plans should be considered, leaving it to the reporter to make the best of whatever situation he finds.

Covering a national election is another major problem of organization. A vast temporary framework of communication with all parts of the country must be set up. Correspondents in strategic places must be obtained and instructed in detail concerning what information to send and when to sent it. This is a task that requires several months. The outline of the campaign is worked out by the managing editor and his assistants put it into effect.

This is the field work. The managing editor must also prepare the internal organization for election night. New, temporary schedules for editors, reporters, copy editors, composing room and pressroom forces must be thought out in detail. Virtually the whole machine must be shifted about for the handling of one vast news story. When this is completed and the machine begins to function on election night, the managing editor takes full charge of the editing, makeup and printing.

The successful managing editor plans to meet difficulties before they arise. He does not rely solely on one plan; he lays alternate plans for use if the most promising fails. If he cannot get the information he wants from one source he gets it from another; if he cannot get it at one time, he does not shelve the idea as impossible, but waits and obtains it when possible.

The function of the principal editors is the selection of news, judging what events are the most vital and most worth covering. This is the managing editor's chief role. He studies events and brings to the newspaper reader news of those that are interesting and important.

THE CHIEF EDITORS

Downward from the managing editor spreads the organization to reporters and correspondents, the gatherers of news, upon whom the whole newspaper structure rests. His immediate assistants are the city, national and foreign editors; the first directs the gathering of the news in the city where the newspaper is published and in its immediate vicinity; the second, the gathering of the news in the United States outside the city of publication; and the third, the gathering of the news in foreign countries. Other editors assisting him are the heads of specialized departments such as financial and business, sports and culture.

On a large morning newspaper there are duplicate editors for day and night to cover the span of the paper's operation, the day editors generally carrying the chief title and the burden of the position. This is by no means the common system, but it illustrates the thorough covering and editing of news by departments; and the functions, if not the individual editors, exist in most city newspaper organizations. For example, most newspapers do not maintain foreign news-gathering facilities, but the function of the foreign editor remains, whether on the day or the night staff. A newspaper that does not have a foreign staff may have a single correspondent in any center abroad, or it may rely on the wire services.

Likewise in the succeeding pages the copy-desk system is divided into three—city, national and foreign—for illustrative purposes, whereas the general practice is either to combine the national and foreign copy desks or to set up a "universal" desk on which all copy is edited.

The City Editor. In the home city of the newspaper and in its vicinity the news-gathering machinery is elaborate. Since the business life of the newspaper is sustained by the community in which it exists, and since the greater part of its circulation is there, local news must be covered in great detail. For the same reason, a substantial part of the news that is printed is of local origin.

At the head of this part of the machine is the city editor. News judgment, executive ability and a store of information of names and events are his chief qualifications. He should know his city, not only its geography but also its history; the masses of its people as well as its important residents. He need not have encyclopedic knowledge, but the background against which he views the world should be broad and human. This is apart from his ability to know news when he hears of it. News judgment is not essentially a thinking process; it is an instinct built upon many things forgotten.

If a local disaster occurs, it is the city editor's task to get reporters to the scene quickly. Not only must they be at the spot, but each also must have a clear idea of the precise part to be played in gathering the details of the event. It is the city editor's function to instruct each person fully and clearly, so that no confusion will result and so that every angle of the story will be covered. Not all the reporters will write what they see or the facts they gather. The editor must pick his best men for that purpose; the others will get information, investigate and report their findings to the men who will organize and write the stories.

For example, a train wreck would be divided into the following angles: the story of the accident itself; stories of eyewitnesses or passengers; the engineer's story; the list of injured, or of the dead and the injured; the color story of the scene; photographs of the scene. In addition, if any were killed, or if any of the injured or dead were important persons, queries would be sent to various places for information regarding them. Here, then, are eight angles, each of which will require at least one reporter and some of them several. Other angles might crop up as information regarding the accident reaches the city editor. If the wreck is a serious one, another reporter would be assigned to write a story of past similar accidents.

The reporter who is to write the lead story of the accident should be sent to the scene if time permits; if time is short, he should remain in the newspaper office and take information by telephone from the reporters on the ground. It is his duty to organize the mass of detail that comes to him. The subsidiary stories are written by the reporters sent to the scene, if they have time to gather the facts and return to the office; otherwise they also telephone the facts to the rewrite staff.

It is a sudden development, like the foregoing illustration, that tests the city editor. It creates a problem that must first be visualized; then a course of action must be mapped out, and then action taken swiftly and with certainty. His plan of campaign depends on the size and abilities of his staff. If he has few reporters, each must be assigned carefully to obtain the best results; if he has many, the task is more easily and more thoroughly accomplished. But if his plan is loose and ill-conceived and the disposition of his men inefficient, the result will be confusion.

The assignment sheet is the city editor's chart. On it is designated each story to be covered and the name of the reporter assigned to cover it. Every reporter is informed daily, usually orally but also by note, what his assignment is to be. This chart serves also as the city editor's record of the disposition of all men under his supervision.

Much news is of spontaneous origin. In such cases the city editor is dependent on his reporters in strategic posts to learn of the event and inform him. He relies also upon the news services and upon outside sources. Any event anywhere is reported eventually in the newspaper office, as well as rumors of much that never happened. In general, however, the newspaper safeguards itself by posting men in places where news ordinarily originates. Future scheduled events are recorded in a "futures" file, on which the city editor relies in the routine of planning assignments. These records may be newspaper clippings, announcements issued by the organizations concerned or publicity agents' copy.

The staff of reporters of a large newspaper may range from a score to a hundred. Many of them are specialists, versed in particular fields, such as public utilities, politics, labor questions, religious matters, science or art; others are feature writers, skilled at describing events colorfully, imparting the flavor as well as reporting the facts; still others are general assignment reporters, able to cover any occurrence efficiently and completely.

There are reporters with fixed assignments or beats, such as those covering the courts, city hall and other public buildings. These men produce most of the day's news, for they are placed in the spots where news ordinarily originates. Other reporters are assigned regularly to police headquarters and to various districts throughout the city; their duty is to report spontaneous stories, to be alert for any news development, and to verify or to cover any angle of stories developing elsewhere.

Suburban correspondents constitute a considerable part of the city editor's staff. They are reporters in outlying towns or cities, often employed directly by the metropolitan newspaper, but usually employed by newspapers in their own communities. The city editor keeps in touch with them by telephone, generally ordering stories but sometimes accepting also those that the correspondent has covered on his own initiative.

National and Foreign Editors. The more the source of news recedes from the home office, the scantier become the means of reporting. Thus the day national and foreign staffs are similar to but far less complex than the day city staff organization. The national and foreign editors act in a supervisory or directing capacity only. Removed from the scenes of action, they can merely advise, or give orders by means of telephone, telegraph or cable.

The larger newspapers have established bureaus or maintain correspondents in many cities of the United States, notably in Washington. The Washington correspondent of a large newspaper is a directing news gatherer, virtually a city editor with a staff of reporters under his control. He is to a large extent independent of the home office and is responsible for covering the news fully in his city.

Spread over the country, however, in all important centers and in many smaller cities, are scores of correspondents who

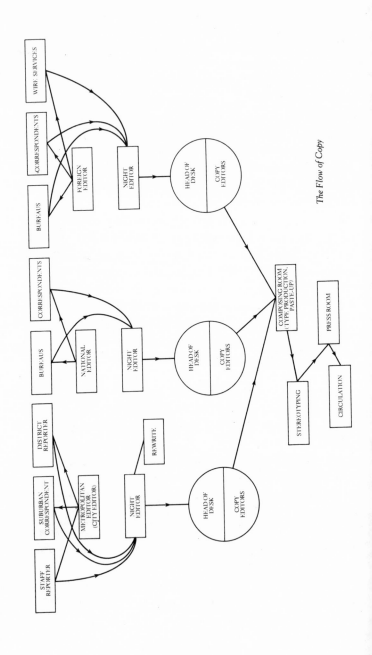

The Flow of Copy

supply stories of news events in their territories only on request, or only after asking the home office whether the story is desired and how much to send. Scanning the domestic field and ordering stories is, in general, the function of the national editor.

In the same manner the foreign editor controls the gathering of news abroad. Still farther from the scene of action, his duties are even more generalized than those of the national editor. As in the case of the Washington correspondent, the heads of bureaus in capitals abroad act as city editors in the cities where they are stationed and as national editors for the countries. Under each is a staff, generally small, of reporters familiar with the country concerned and with its politics and language. The foreign editor in the home office exercises general oversight over the whole foreign field. Not the least of his duties is keeping watch on the skeletonizing by correspondents abroad of cable copy, which, when properly done, may save the newspaper many thousands of dollars yearly in cable tolls.

THE "NIGHT SIDE" OF A MORNING NEWSPAPER

These chief editors gather or direct the gathering of most of the news. In the late afternoon the "night side," whose functions are to edit and to print the newspaper, takes control.

Each editor is duplicated at night by an editor whose duties are similar, although modern practice is to fix hours of duty so that the responsible executive is available during the vital hours of news gathering and editing. Thus there is an over-all night executive, usually called the news editor, with a number of assistants, varying with the size of the newspaper, who exercises general control over the gathering of news of events happening at night and over the editing, placing and printing of all news stories.

The process of "taking over" by the night staff is important, since it is vital that no break occur between the day and the night activities. In the case of the city editor, this is accomplished by the transferring of the assignment sheet by the day editor to his night counterpart, the record itself being supplemented by oral explanations of the covering or the treatment of stories. In the case of the national and foreign editors, no personal transfer takes place except in special situations, but the night men, by scanning the messages that have been sent and received, obtain a picture of what has been done during the day.

The Night Editors. Assuming all the responsibilities of the city editor, his night assistant in addition has control of the writing of most of the news, including that covered during the day, a function little exercised by the day executive. He tells the reporter how much space he may have and, if necessary, how to construct the story.

His staff is supplemented also by reporters covering specified districts, duplicating the day system, and by rewrite men who take the facts of stories over the telephone from district men or correspondents and who write the stories. The latter usually take advantage of shorthand or symbols developed by themselves to facilitate the process of getting news by telephone. Generally they have been graduated from the ranks of reporters and frequently have unusual gifts of imagination. To draw out a story from the reporter at the scene, to organize it in the mind quickly, to grasp at once its news features and value, require experience and ingenuity of a high order.

Under the night editor's direction also is the city copy desk, made up of a head of the desk and copy editors. With the night editor begins the process of editing the news, which is continued to completion by the copy editors.

A similar system is in effect for both the national and foreign staffs. For these night editors the foreign and domestic bureaus and correspondents make up the reporting staffs. The aid of reporters on the night city staff, however, is frequently asked by these editors to rewrite a story that is not properly written by their correspondents and to provide background material from clippings or other sources for out-of-town stories.

Afternoon newspapers have the same general organization, as to function at any rate. But their problems differ and are multiplied because they are reporting, editing and publishing during the day hours when news events are occurring. Assignments of their reporting staff are similar to those of morning newspaper procedure but the bulk of their news content is produced by rewrite men from facts telephoned by reporters at the scene. They must keep up, edition by edition, with developments as they occur. They work by telephone largely, shift their display of stories as their staff reports, play the "spot news" hard. They lack time for a moderate period of reflection and judgment of the relative value of news occurrences. Their executive staff also is less elaborate than that of the large morning paper, the functions being concentrated in fewer men.

The remaining important night executive is the makeup editor. As the liaison between the news room and the composing room, he has authority in both departments and is subordinate only to the night editor in charge and his assistants. His chief concerns are to place stories properly in reference to the space required by advertisements and to typographical appearance, and to get the paper to press on time. Working from dummy pages that indicate the placing and the space occupied by display advertisements and from schedules or proofs of news stories, he organizes the page layouts and indicates to the composing-room paste-up force where the news stories are to appear. The dressing up of the newspaper to make the display of news attractive depends upon the makeup editor and his assistants.

Late in the afternoon city reporters return to the office prepared to record in news stories the events of the day. Over the cable wires and through the air by radio telephone comes the record of the day's happenings from the foreign bureaus. By telegraph, telephone, and over leased wires begin to flash the stories of events in the domestic field.

The electronic system of handling hard copy of news stories, described in some detail in chapter 4, has eliminated the vast flood of manuscript copy into the hands of editors. Instead, the "copy" is stored in the computers' banks and any individual story can be recalled from these banks for judgment by the various editors and for detailed editing by computer at the various copy desks.

A system of summaries has been devised as one method of keeping a record of the important stories. Under this system, the city editor requires each reporter to summarize in 50 to 100 words the main points of his assignment. The national editor receives from the Washington bureau schedules summarizing briefly all stories of importance that will be filed; for other stories he relies on the information contained in the orders sent out by the day editor. Owing to the cost of foreign messages, no schedules are sent from the foreign bureaus, but the same purpose is served by summaries written on the foreign copy desk.

The whole editing process is governed by the amount of space available for news. Taking into consideration the number of columns of advertising matter, the higher night editors determine the total allotment for news. The number of pages

Organization of the Newspaper

PUBLISHER

NEWS DEPT.
- EXECUTIVE EDITOR
- MANAGING EDITOR
- DEPUTY MANAGING EDITOR
- NEWS EDITOR

- METROPOLITAN EDITOR
  - REPORTERS
  - REWRITE
  - NIGHT EDITOR
  - COPY DESK

- NATIONAL EDITOR
  - BUREAUS AND CORRESPONDENTS
  - NIGHT EDITOR
  - COPY DESK

- FOREIGN EDITOR
  - BUREAUS AND CORRESPONDENTS
  - NIGHT EDITOR
  - COPY DESK

SPECIALIZED NEWS
- FINANCIAL AND BUSINESS, TRANSPORTATION — COPY DESK
- CULTURE (ART, DRAMA, MUSIC, MOVIES) — COPY DESK
- FAMILY/STYLE (SOCIETY, COOKING, HEALTH) — COPY DESK
- SCIENCE
- REAL ESTATE
- SPORTS — COPY DESK

PROMOTION DEPT.
- PROMOTION MANAGER

ADVERTISING DEPT.
- BUSINESS MANAGER
- ADVERTISING DIRECTOR

MECHANICAL DEPT.
- MECHANICAL SUPERINTENDENT
  - COMPOSING ROOM FOREMAN
  - PRESS ROOM FOREMAN

CIRCULATION DEPT.
- CIRCULATION DIRECTOR

SUNDAY DEPT.
- SUNDAY EDITOR
  - MAGAZINE
  - BOOK REVIEW
  - SPECIAL SECTIONS

for an issue is fixed in consultation with the advertising department and is normally based on past experience for the day or season. The average news content tends to become standardized. The ratio of advertising to news is variable, and it is neither a good business nor a good editorial policy to establish a fixed ratio. The tendency is to expand the newspaper when the volume of news and of advertising is large and to contract it when the volume of both is small. If, however, the volume of advertising is small, the news space is not necessarily reduced in order to keep down the size of the paper. The size is fixed by daily conditions. In most offices the minimum routine requirement for news space stays at about the same level and is rarely cut drastically; on the other hand it frequently is expanded if the news volume makes that course necessary.

The space allotted for news is divided among city, national and foreign editors, each receiving approximately the amount that he estimates he will require. Each editor is guided by this allotment in judging the space that may be given to any story.

SUPPLEMENTARY DEPARTMENTS

In the estimate of total news columns, allowance must be made also for other departments, operating semi-independently of the news department, but under the supervision of the night editors. Among these are the sports department, made up of reporters versed in sports matters and specialized copy editors; the financial and business department, composed of writers and copy editors who are authorities in their field; the culture department, made up of drama, motion picture, ballet, music, art and book critics and reporters of news in each of these fields.

The divisions range from one-man departments on smaller newspapers to departments employing a score or more persons, each with a specialized task, on the large newspapers. The division of the newspaper organization depends entirely upon its size and resources. The news of each department may be edited by semi-independent copy desks made up of special copy editors, but usually all copy goes to the general copy desks and is edited in the same manner as general news copy. The product of all these departments is news and differs not at all from general news in importance. News is departmentalized solely to facilitate gathering and to insure expert treatment. Allotment of space for departmental news is made at the same time as that for general news.

Space must be allotted also for pictures, the amount depending on the newspaper's policy. If news pictures or photographs of persons are desired, a news picture service, perhaps maintained by the newspaper itself, supplies them, and the cuts are made either by the newspaper's own art department or by outside plants specializing in such work.

THE FRONT PAGE

From the great number of stories that enter the newspaper office in a single night, six to ten or more must be selected for the front page. In some offices this responsibility falls upon one of the assistants to the night editor in charge, and it is to facilitate his work that the summaries of news stories are kept. In other offices the conference system is used, under which the city, national and foreign editors confer with the higher executives, and recommend for the first page their chief stories. In this case, summaries are unnecessary.

Many stories are obviously page one stories; others are doubtful. On the latter, conferences may be held by the editor in charge of the task with his colleagues or superior. If there are more stories of sufficient importance to be displayed on the front page than space permits, they must be weighed against one another.

The right-hand side above the fold of the paper is the best display space because that quarter of the newspaper can be seen if the paper is folded on the newsstand. The editor who selects page one stories must consider balance also, and so place one-column and two-column boxes, pictures, maps and other typographical devices so that the display is attractive. This is especially important when the lead story requires a headline that spreads over two, three, or more columns. Such a layout frequently alters the display value of the columns and requires special care in balancing the whole page. Balance does not necessarily mean regularity, which may serve only to diminish the display value of the whole page. In addition to the chief stories selected for page one, minor short stories may also be used to break up long columns of type or to give a pleasing effect of irregularity.

The front page of a morning newspaper may not change from first edition to last, but the afternoon newspaper, with perhaps six editions, is likely to change the page one makeup for each edition. This is because the afternoon paper is being published while most of the day's news events are occurring and continual shifting of stories is necessary to keep pace with events. The early or "bulldog" edition of an afternoon newspaper may contain chiefly the same stories that appeared in the late editions of the morning newspapers in a rewritten form. As new events occur, however, the early stories are shifted from the first page to the inside of the paper and from the forward pages to the back, until finally the least important drop out and the more important are retained on less conspicuous pages, unless new developments enhance their value.

THE COMPOSING ROOM

The old-time composing room, in which the outstanding feature was an array of linotype machines, for nearly a century the backbone of the publishing industry, has almost disappeared with the advent of the computer. The striking element now is the long rows of tables, desks and racks for pasting up page forms of proofs typeset by the computer, plus various electronic machines for producing plates for the printing presses.

THE DEADLINE APPROACHES

By the time the page one makeup has been determined, the deadline for the first edition is approaching. Dummies of the front page go to the city, national and foreign editors and to the makeup editor. Guided by it, the copy desks write the proper headlines for the designated stories.

Working from proofs, schedules from the various desks, and instructions from the news editors, the makeup staff dummies pages as quickly as possible and sends them to the paste-up staff in the composing room where other makeup people supervise the operation.

The makeup work proceeds in relays by fixed schedule. Some newspapers set an early deadline for the financial news so that the back pages are out of the way when the rush of general news makeup begins. The schedule may call for the completion of from four to sixteen page forms every twenty minutes, depending on the number of pages in the issue and on the newspaper's size and facilities.

The first page form usually is the last to be filled. At times pages are held for a few minutes in order to get into the first edition a last-minute story, but delay is avoided when possible. The time of the deadline has been set to meet circulation requirements, and a few minutes lost in the composing room may cause tardy deliveries at trains for distribution in the suburbs and elsewhere.

The First Edition. After the first edition deadline has been passed, a temporary lull settles on the news room. Then the vibration of the great presses can be felt. In a few minutes the first edition, still wet and smelling of printer's ink, comes up from the pressroom. It is corrected, cut and added to. The second edition is the next goal. It appears soon afterward, and the first is already history.

If the organization of a large newspaper seems to be so complex as to be bewildering, it can be pointed out that this complexity is more apparent that real. The functions are simple. The editor of a small paper in a county seat does the same work on a smaller scale. If he solicits his own advertising, he is functioning as the business department. He is his own reporter, collecting and writing local news; he is the copy editor and headline writer; he is the managing editor and makeup editor; the editorial writer and probably the compositor and printer and pressman and distributor. If he has correspondents throughout the county and a state or national wire service he is a national editor; and if his paper is large enough to have a fuller world service, he becomes a foreign editor also.

If his paper should grow, requiring the adding of employees, he would begin the division of labor, and the functions of gathering, editing and printing news would be distributed among several persons. He would meet new conditions with a more complex organization, just as the large newspaper expands its structure to meet the conditions of keen competition and demands for speed.

2. THE COPY EDITOR

ERRORS creep into newspaper copy from many sources. News passes through many hands; it is garbled in transmission; it is written and rewritten by men of varied ages, education and temperament; it is read and edited under similar conditions. Wrong perspective or partisanship, too much enthusiasm or too little, may handicap a story. The very speed with which newspapers must be printed permits mistakes to slip by the many persons who handle news in its course through the news machine. The continuous struggle of the newspaper is to eliminate errors. Many checks have been set up against them and the chief of these is the copy editor.

THE IMPORTANCE OF THE COPY EDITOR

The copy editor is virtually the last man between his newspaper and the public. The copy may have been read several times before it reaches him, but its ultimate form, phraseology and spirit rest in his hands. Mistakes or poor writing that pass him are almost certain to reach the reader in print. They may be detected in the office in time to be corrected, but many such blunders are never discovered except by the newspaper reader.

The greatest weapon of the copy editor in his efforts to eliminate errors is an alertness that challenges every fact, every name, virtually every word. Every fact should be checked. Those that appear incorrect and cannot be verified must be

its that are absurd or dangerous are de-
n. Likewise the facts should be weighed
to assure consistency.

ie copy editor is critical, not creative. In
iould he rewrite a story completely. If it
ept by being rewritten, that work should
be done by _____ e man or by the reporter who wrote the original story. The desk man must cope with the material that is given him and make the most of it by recasting, striking out superfluous words, substituting active or colorful words for dead ones, expressing a phrase in a word and by other similar means.

The finished product should be concise, forceful, complete. This should be the copy editor's aim with every story, not merely with the important ones. A great news story virtually tells itself; it is the brief stories that most often are allowed to slip by without careful editing. Any story can be improved, even though the editing consists of transposing a word, shifting a punctuation mark, substituting a concrete word for a general one, or an Anglo-Saxon verb for a Latin one.

Leaving unaltered one word that should be changed is not a trivial matter. The careful copy editor leaves nothing to chance. His object is not only to correct errors, but also to improve.

With a unanimity that is somewhat disconcerting to the copy editor, reporters profess to regard him as a mutilator of good copy, and there is some ground for this opinion. There are some desk men temperamentally unfitted to make the most of another man's writing; their conception of what a story should be is so strong that virtual rewriting is the only course they can follow. Such men must be restrained, and, if they remain copy editors, trained to the editorial viewpoint rather than to the reportorial. The general aim of the copy desk is to preserve as far as possible the words of the reporter, if they express what he desires to convey, and to retain the spirit imparted by him, if it is proper. As the final link in a long and expensive process, the copy editor can destroy the honest work of many reporters.

The business of writing and editing news is a cooperative undertaking, demanding the best of many brains. There is no place for pride of authorship. The desk man should recognize and retain the merits of the story given to him to edit; the reporter should realize that the copy editor often saves him from grave mistakes and generally improves his work.

The Copy Desk. The copy desk usually is U-shaped. The head of the desk sits at the center of the curve; his position is known as the "slot," and he himself, sometimes, as the "slot man." The copy editors sit "on the rim."

The head of the desk brings to his computer screen from the storage banks each story in the local report, reads it to form an opinion of the required headline information, edits it as closely as he wishes, and passes it to one of the copy editors, who calls the story to his own computer screen. When the copy has been edited in detail and headlined, it is returned to the head of the desk. If the edited copy and the headline meet with his approval, both are sent to the composing room. If there is criticism of either, the necessary corrections are made in the copy or the headline is rewritten or rephrased.

In giving copy to his editors the head of the desk takes into consideration their abilities or their special knowledge. Like reporters, there are some who are experts in special fields, such as politics, labor questions, railroads, art or literature; others are especially adept at writing feature headlines and still others are able to cope with stories of any kind. Some are slow, careful editors; others are quick as well as accurate. Speed is a necessity when the deadline draws near.

How the copy editor deals with copy and headlines is described at length in subsequent chapters. His approach to the task depends largely on his abilities. A good method in the case of a long or a complicated story is to read the copy once simply for information and to gain a general idea of its structure. Probably in this reading any obvious inconsistencies in facts or faults in construction will be detected and corrected, by editing in the former case and by rearrangement in the latter. The next step is a second reading for close editing, with attention to the standards set forth later. A third reading of the edited copy, while not necessary in many instances, is an additional safeguard to assure a product as finished as it lies in the power of the copy editor to achieve.

Not until the copy has been carefully corrected is the copy editor in a position to consider the headline. His alterations may modify the point of view or qualify the statement of the facts in such a way that a headline built on the original copy would have been incorrect or distorted. When the editing is completed it is often helpful as preparation for writing the headline for the editor mentally to stand away from the story so that he may view it as a whole rather than in detail. This method is not necessarily to determine the news point, which at this stage should be obvious, but to discover the most effective way to tell the news in the headline; whether, for example, to write a broad, all-inclusive headline or a narrow, more specific one that singles out one phase of the story.

The Copy Editor's Background. The education, experience and knowledge of the copy editor cannot be too broad. The more he has learned, seen or knows, the greater his value to the newspaper. He should have a wide knowledge of names, places and events; he must be well-informed in the arts, sciences and social trends; he should know history and literature and be familiar with the machinery of governments and law.

It is imperative that he be acquainted with his own city, if he is an editor of local copy. He must know its geography, its people, its government, its officials, its buildings. If he is an editor of national copy, he must have a wide knowledge of national politics, movements, figures and events. Copy editors dealing with legislation in the national or in state capitals should have detailed information about the machinery of legislatures. If the editor is dealing with foreign copy he must know much about the politics, economics and government of the countries concerned and of their recent history at least. Finally the copy editor must have common sense. The logic he uses to test the reasonableness of assertions in news stories is the same logic he applies in everyday affairs.

THE VALUE OF REFERENCE BOOKS

Whatever the store of information, memory cannot always be trusted. It is necessary to verify. Familiarity with the common reference books is invaluable to the copy editor. If he does not know or cannot recall a name, a date, or any other fact, he should know where they can be found. It is worthwhile for every copy editor to investigate the reference shelves of his office so that he can put his hand on the proper book quickly. Most newspapers have "morgues" where newspaper and sometimes other clippings concerning events and persons are filed. Many questions of fact can be determined quickly by reference to these clippings. Some newspapers also have libraries where difficulties on questions more remote than those ordinarily arising in editorial work can be settled. Newspapers may also have access to computer retrieval systems such as the New York Times Information Bank.

Some of the more common reference books are the following:

DICTIONARIES (Not only for definitions and spelling, but also for historical names and dates. Foreign dictionaries are often helpful.)

ENCYCLOPEDIAS

TELEPHONE DIRECTORIES (for spelling of names and for home locations)

CITY DIRECTORIES (for spelling of names, home locations and businesses)

THE COLUMBIA-LIPPINCOTT GAZETTEER (for place names, locations and geographical descriptions)

OFFICIAL STANDARD NAMES GAZETTEERS OF THE UNITED STATES BOARD OF GEOGRAPHIC NAMES

THE WORLD ALMANAC (for general factual information)

NEW YORK TIMES INDEX

WHO'S WHO

WHO'S WHO IN AMERICA

WHO'S WHO IN NEW YORK

WHO'S WHO IN CANADA

WHO'S WHO IN AUSTRALIA

WHO'S WHO IN ART

WHO'S WHO IN LABOR

WHO'S WHO IN GOVERNMENT (statesmen of the world)

WHO'S WHO IN FINANCE AND INDUSTRY

WHO'S WHO IN FRANCE

WER IST WER? (Who's Who of Germany)

THE EUROPA YEARBOOK

STATESMAN'S YEAR BOOK

YEAR BOOK OF AGRICULTURE

AMERICAN YEAR BOOK (record of events and progress)

AMERICAN MEN AND WOMEN OF SCIENCE

STATISTICAL ABSTRACT OF THE UNITED STATES

HISTORICAL STATISTICS OF THE UNITED STATES

LEGISLATIVE MANUAL (New York State)

BURKE'S PEERAGE, BARONETAGE, KNIGHTAGE (names and ranks of the Royal Family and the British nobility)

DEBRETT'S PEERAGE, BARONETAGE, KNIGHTAGE AND COMPANIONAGE SOCIAL
    REGISTER (names and family connections of prominent persons)
STANDARD AND POOR'S REGISTER
MOODY'S BANK AND FINANCE MANUAL
MOODY'S INDUSTRIAL MANUAL
MOODY'S PUBLIC UTILITY MANUAL
MOODY'S TRANSPORTATION MANUAL
DIRECTORY OF DIRECTORS (officers of corporations in New York)
JANE'S FIGHTING SHIPS (general and technical information about war-
    ships throughout the world)
JANE'S ALL THE WORLD'S AIRCRAFT
ARMY REGISTER (list of officers, active and retired)
NAVY REGISTER
LLOYD'S REGISTER OF SHIPPING (names and facts about commercial
    ships)
RECORD OF THE AMERICAN BUREAU OF SHIPPING
AYER DIRECTORY OF PUBLICATIONS
WORKING PRESS OF THE NATION
WILLING'S PRESS GUIDE
STATISTICS SOURCES

The habit of reading newspapers, particularly their own, is necessary to copy editors as well as to editors and reporters. To know what the new development of a continuing story is, one must know what has been printed. It seems elementary that the newspaper man should know what is in his own newspaper, but many are careless in this respect. The copy editor who does not read it thoroughly it not competent to handle a news story acceptably.

This is especially true for students of journalism. Intelligent reading of the newspapers is the groundwork for any progress they may hope to make in the profession. It is impossible to learn anything about newspapers unless they are read for information and analyzed for technical knowledge.

It is taken for granted that the copy editor knows English grammar and how to write good English. Something more

should be required. He should be a student of language because he is to a great extent its guardian. Colloquialisms and
slang that are ordinary in speech should be permitted to appear
infrequently in newspaper writing. The ultimate value of the
copy editor rests solely on his conception of what purpose his
newspaper must serve and his ability to help it achieve that
end.

3. EDITING THE COPY

THE MISTAKES common to all copy are those of word usage, spelling, punctuation and grammar.

The English used in the newspaper should be that common to all well-educated persons. Language divides naturally into four groups: literary, common, colloquial and slang. Common usage is preferred, because it sets a single standard; the literary is too stilted, although the tendency probably should be toward the literary rather than the colloquial. Slang generally is to be barred.

Discrimination in the use of words is an art. The synonym is convenient but dangerous, and it should be employed with great care. If the copy editor substitutes "assert" for "say," a common practice to obtain variety, he has altered the meaning perceptibly. There is a word to express every action, thought or emotion and it can be found with little difficulty. Synonyms must be used more freely in writing headlines, because of a "rule" against repeating words, but in copy no such freedom should be permitted. Variety can be achieved in many other ways than by abusing the synonym.

Attempts at "fine" or literary writing often lead the reporter into triteness. A few such hackneyed phrases are:

abreast of the times	order out of chaos
was the recipient of	breathless silence
sigh of relief	effect an entrance
in social circles	goes without saying
dull sickening thud	lingering illness

located his whereabouts
news leaked out
much in evidence
beat a hasty retreat
in the business world
was an impressive sight
sadder but wiser
deafening crash
general public

inclement weather
limped into port
lodged in jail
made good his escape
summoned medical aid
blunt instrument
take into custody
crowded to capacity

There are scores of others. The copy editor should change them.

It is absurd also to strain to avoid repetition of words, particularly names; as "capital city" for Washington; "Bay State" for Massachusetts; "the Western metropolis" for any large city in the West.

Directness and simplicity are the easiest ways to avoid such expressions.

PUNCTUATION

Punctuation promotes clarity when properly used. Sentences that need little punctuation, however, are in general the better. To indicate the need of commas and how their use can alter meaning, the following sentences may be studied:

The boys and girls who were on the ground floor escaped.
The boys and girls, who were on the ground floor, escaped.

The man who is an atheist will be imprisoned.
The man, who is an atheist, will be imprisoned.

Fifty delegates who live in New York will be sent.
Fifty delegates, who live in New York, will be sent.

The woman who is a singer is happy.
The woman, who is a singer, is happy.

The mistakes of punctuation most frequent in newspaper copy occur in the use of quotation marks. Every quotation must be closed and the copy editor, on seeing an opening quotation mark, must be certain that the quoted matter is ended with a quotation mark. Quoted passages such as the following appear often in newspapers:

He said he thought it was "now more important than ever for our country to demand the tightest possible monitoring and control of spent nuclear fuels, but a prerequisite for success in this program is a consistent struggle to control nuclear weapons through the stategic arms limitation process. We simply must prove to doubting nations that we will do our part in controlling the atomic arms race so that the others can be induced not to join it. As a matter of fact, this is required under the nuclear nonproliferation treaty which we have pledged to honor."

Although this practice is defensible, the better method is to edit the passage as follows:

He said he thought it was "now more important than ever for our country to demand the tightest possible monitoring and control of spent nuclear fuels, but a prerequisite for success in this program is a consistent struggle to control nuclear weapons through the strategic arms limitation process."

"We simply must prove to doubting nations that we will do our part in controlling the atomic arms race so that others can be induced not to join it," he continued. "As a matter of fact, this is required under the nonproliferation treaty which we have pledged to honor."

It is well to end quoted matter introduced by "he said that" with the phrase, clause or sentence so introduced. Not only does it make the writing clear and more effective, but it also follows the general newspaper rule to set off quoted matter by paragraphs so that it draws attention.

GRAMMAR

Mistakes in grammar are of such variety that the copy editor or the student of journalism must be referred to the grammar books, if he does not have a working knowledge of the rules.

The more common blunders, for which the copy editor must be alert, are these:

Disagreement in Number Between Subject and Verb. Frequently the verb occurs so far away from the subject that the singular form is used when the subject is plural, or the plural form when the subject is singular. Again confusion may arise when the subject is a clause or when the subject is, for example, "one of the members," or like phrases. The incorrect verbs should be noted in the following illustrations:

The cross-examination of the witness by the defense and the ruling by the court on the admissibility of his evidence *was* put off until tomorrow.

In outlining a set of recommendations for the industry to solve its problems, he warned those who still believe the industry will survive, even if not one of his recommendations *are* carried out, that there is no escaping the truth. . . .

Dangling Participles. In the following illustrations, the first sentence is incorrect, the second and third correct:

Having summed up for two hours, a recess was ordered and the lawyer left.

Having summed up for two hours, the lawyer left after a recess had been ordered.

After he had summed up for two hours, a recess was ordered and the lawyer left.

In the following the dangling participle is at the end:

The two prisoners made a complaint at the station house where they were taken by the policeman alleging extortion.

It should read:

The two prisoners made a complaint, alleging extortion, at the station house where they were taken by the policeman.

Sequence of Tenses. The copy editor should keep close watch on the governing verb (that of the main news story) and relate the tenses of other verbs to it, as determined by the obvious or implied time sequence. The time of the main news story is almost always placed in the past tense. The historical present has become obsolete in newspaper writing.

When the governing verb is in the past, the verbs in clauses dependent upon it also take past tense, even though the idea of past time does not need to be introduced into the clause. This fact should be kept in mind, for no rule is more commonly violated in newspaper writing. This sequence is called normal sequence, and while the present, or vivid sequence, is often retained in speech, it is not good newspaper practice. For example: "He said that he is well-to-do," is permissible; but "He said that he was well-to-do" is the normal sequence and preferable in newspaper writing.

In the news story the events related almost always are previous in time to that of the governing verb, which, generally, is in the past tense. Therefore, many of the verbs will be necessarily in the past perfect tense to show previous time. In this example the tenses in the clauses are incorrect:

He testified that he saw the accused man at the scene but that his suspicions were not aroused.

It is obvious that the events the witness is telling about are previous to the time at which he is telling about them. The sentence should read:

He testified that he had seen the accused man at the scene but that his suspicions had not been aroused.

Frequently this construction is met with in newspaper writing:

He saw the accused man at the scene, he testified, but his suspicions were not aroused.

This is correct. It would be incorrect to write this sentence in this way:

He had seen the accused man at the scene, he testified, but his suspicions had not been aroused.

The reason is that the words "he testified" are parenthetical and are not, in this case, those that govern the tense sequence of the other parts of the sentence. In the first case the facts asserted by the witness are clauses, and the tenses are governed by "he testified." In the second case, they are not clauses and are not governed by the parenthetical "he testified."

The normal sequence has one exception. When the fact set forth in the clause is permanently true, the tense of the clause is not governed by the main verb. For example, one says:

He said that the world is round (not was round).

In keeping the proper relation between the main verb and subordinate verb forms, an infinitive construction should have the present tense unless it represents action prior to that of the governing verb. It is incorrect to write:

It was unfortunate for him to have testified that he had seen the accused man at the scene.

It should read:

It was unfortunate for him to testify that he had seen the accused man at the scene.

A common mistake is to use a present participle in conjunction with a verb in the past tense. Here is an example:

Falling four stories and crashing through a skylight, John Jones, a painter, was saved from serious injury yesterday when he landed on a stack of books.

It should read:

Having fallen four stories and (having) crashed through a skylight, John Jones, a painter, was saved from serious injury yesterday when he landed on a stack of books.

False Passive or "Was Given" Construction. The subject in the active form of a sentence represents the actor, and the object, the receiver of the action; also, when the active form is changed to the passive, the receiver of the action becomes the subject, and the actor, if expressed, is represented as the object of a preposition. When a sentence in the active form contains both a direct and an indirect object, mistakes often are made in giving the passive construction. Frequently the indirect object in the active form is used as the subject in the passive form, but this makes an incorrect construction known as the false passive. Note these sentences. Active: *They gave him their heartfelt thanks for his trouble.* False passive: *He was given their heartfelt thanks for his trouble.* True passive: *Their heartfelt thanks were given to him for his trouble.* The first sentence contains both a direct and an indirect object. The direct object is the noun *thanks* and the indirect object is the pronoun *him.* In the second sentence it will be observed that the subject is represented by the word that is the indirect object in the active form of the sentence, and the predicate verb, which is passive, seems to be followed by an object. The third sentence shows the true passive form.

Pronouns and Antecedents. The copy editor should be vigilant to eliminate the pronoun "it" from copy, because the word almost always leaves the intent ambiguous. When repeating a subject is necessary for clarity, repeat it or rephrase the sentence. Likewise, when several persons are mentioned in one sentence, the pronouns "he" and "she" should be avoided unless it is unmistakable what subject is intended. However, if the meaning is clear, the copy editor should not hesitate to strike out a noun and write a pronoun when the repetition of the noun makes the sentence awkward. Note the ambiguity of pronouns in the following:

After the Governor and the Lieutenant-Governor had conferred for two hours concerning the advisability of levying additional taxes to balance the budget, *he* announced that a decision would be made within a week.

When the questioning of the witness had been completed, it was said at the District Attorney's office that the case would be laid before the grand jury next week only if *it* could be speeded.

TYPOGRAPHICAL STYLE

Every newspaper of standing has its own style for the spelling of many words, for abbreviations and for capitalization, and also special rules governing the quotation of titles of books, plays, songs, etc.

Some examples of variation of spelling are the following:

dominos	dominoes	criticize	criticise
buses	busses	controller	comptroller
catalogue	catalog	anesthetic	anaesthetic
gray	grey	ax	axe
disk	disc	calibre	caliber
gibe	jibe	pretense	pretence
plow	plough	theatre	theater
vendor	vender	glamour	glamor
referenda	referendums		

There are wide differences in capitalization also. Many newspapers capitalize "President" when it stands alone and refers to the President of the United States; and all other titles when they stand alone and refer to a particular man, such as "the Governor," "the Mayor," and "the Senator" (but "the governors," "the mayors" and "the senators"). Street is capitalized when it refers to Wall Street, but some newspapers lower-case the "s" when street is part of an address.

Concerning abbreviations, it should be noted that some occur in headlines, where brevity is essential, but are not permitted in copy. Some of those permitted in copy are "Gov." for Governor, when followed by the name; "Col." for colonel (and most other military titles when followed by the name); but not "Pres." for President, nor "Sen." for Senator, even in headlines. It is permitted to abbreviate long names of organizations, such as UNESCO, A.F.L.-C.I.O and F.C.C., but this practice is restricted to organizations whose names are thoroughly familiar to readers.

Some newspapers quote the titles of books, plays, songs and pictures; others do not. Still others quote some but not all. The stylebook of the newspaper is the only guide in these cases and the copy editor should be familiar with its contents.

ERRORS OF FACT

The constant effort of the newspaper is to detect and to correct or eliminate errors of fact. To this end the copy and the proofs are examined by many persons; but on the copy editor falls the chief burden. Such mistakes are most frequent in dates, locations, and in the characterization or description of past events.

A distinction should be made between current events and those that are a matter of record. In the present, the facts of a situation may not be fully established. For example, the newspaper may print a story, based on the most accurate information available at the moment, saying that the victim of a murder was shot at Avenue X and Fifteenth Street. The following day, the case having been further clarified, the story may say that the victim was shot in his apartment at Avenue

A and Sixtieth Street, and thrown into the street at the place where he was found. Such variation as this cannot be considered in the same light as in cases where the facts are fully known and recorded. This does not mean, however, that every effort should not be made to establish the truth of the statements in every story, no matter how minor it may appear in relation to other news. Serious consequences may follow from the printing of an incorrect name or address.

In past events, however, the facts are a matter of record. In the following illustrations several mistakes are made, any one of which might occur in a news story:

The disaster recalled the sinking of the Titanic on April 14–15, 1915, in which 1,513 lives were lost after the American liner hit an iceberg in the North Atlantic.

Seven years after the first American flight into space, U.S. Astronaut Neil R. Armstrong, commander of the Apollo 11 mission, became the first man to set foot on the moon on July 20, 1968.

Every fact and figure in these examples should be suspected by the copy editor and checked. After reference to an almanac containing records such as these or to the "morgue" clippings, he would edit the sentences as follows:

The disaster recalled the sinking of the Titanic on April 14–15, 1912, in which 1,513 lives were lost after the British liner hit an iceberg in the North Atlantic.

Eight years after the first American flight into space, U.S. Astronaut Neil A. Armstrong, commander of the Apollo 11 mission, became the first man to set foot on the moon on July 20, 1969.

The facts of a story must be consistent. If those in one paragraph contradict or cast doubt upon those in another paragraph, a change must be made in one case or the other. If the route of a robber's flight is described in one part of the story, he cannot be permitted to flee by any other route in another part of the story. Should the lead of the story say that the Mayor denounced waste in the city departments, the language of his statement must be, in fact, denunciatory. If he mildly criticizes only or suggests reforms, the lead must so describe his action. Each news story is a problem in clear, logical presentation.

Here is an example of an inconsistent lead:

Angered by criticism of "extravagance" in the city government, Mayor Blank denounced waste of the taxpayers' money before the city council yesterday and demanded that retrenchments be made "all along the line." He warned the heads of departments that 25 percent reductions should be made in requests for funds in the next budget and that if drastic cuts were not made he might discover ways to make them. The Mayor spoke heatedly for twenty minutes and left the meeting abruptly. Action on several important measures had been on the calendar, but all were put over until the next session on Tuesday.

"I have heard much criticism of the cost of the government of the city," said the Mayor. "This criticism must be stopped by efforts to reduce expenditures all along the line. The President of the Board of Trade declares that, with a little effort, slashes of as much as 25 percent can be made in the next budget. Perhaps it can be done. If you cannot do it, I may find ways to do it. If we fail, we can let our critics point the way.

"The taxpayers' money must not be wasted. Every dollar of it must be spent carefully and a dollar's worth of service obtained for it. But I am tired of continual attacks on this administration by persons who do not realize the mounting cost of every city department."

Such misrepresentation as is contained in the phrases "denounced waste" and "demanded retrenchments" might easily occur if an attempt is made to "sensationalize" the story. In the foregoing, the Mayor's words can certainly be interpreted as a warning and as a retort to his critics, but no more. The copy editor must soften the terms used to bring the lead into conformity with the quoted statement.

The copy editor must know how to construct a story and must understand the importance of making the lead or introduction attract the attention of the reader.

There are two kinds of leads: one which puts the climax first, summarizing the important facts in the first few paragraphs; and the "delayed" lead, or feature-story lead, that works up to the climax later in the story. The first kind is the more common; it tells the news immediately and forcefully. The second, reserved for special types of stories, sets the mood and reaches the news point at a later stage.

This lead illustrates the direct method:

> Tears, fainting spells and charges of "backbiting" and "politics" marked the final judgments on the show prizes of the thirtieth annual show of the Atlantic Cat Club yesterday. Although the judges reached quick decisions for most of the eight prizes awarded, a three-hour discussion and the services of a series of referees were required to settle whether a black cat with green eyes or a red cat of unknown parentage deserved the title of best novice and the accompanying $25 prize.

Here is a delayed, or feature-story, lead:[1]

> Up six flights of stairs at 129 East Ninety-seventh Street, turn right in the gloomy hall and ring the bell on John Costen's door. You hear the soft, brushing movement of a hand on the inside panel, a fumbling on the knob and the door opens. John Costen has been blind for years.
>
> But he was cheerful last night. Something like animation brightened the sightless gray eyes as he told about Dick, who swallowed the poker. Dick is his pet collie. Spends hours with him at the news stand on the northeast corner of Lexington Avenue and Ninety-sixth Street. Dick will be back from the hospital today.
>
> "Best dog in the world," said Costen, "but maybe a little too active. He's only a year old, you see. Two weeks ago he was playing around

---

[1] By the late Meyer Berger of *The New York Times*.

here in the kitchen. I couldn't see him, of course. He reaches up and grabs the stove poker in his mouth and the handle comes off. A wire at the end of it got caught in Dick's tongue and, trying to get rid of that, he kept swallowing more and more of the handle."

One of the neighbors rushed Dick to a veterinarian in Yorkville, but he could not help. And there was the collie with a piece of iron six inches long and one inch around in his innards. He was taken to the Ellen Prince Speyer Hospital for Animals.

"They took an X-ray picture of him right away," Costen said, "and a friend of mine said it looked pretty bad, but Dr. Meyer, the veterinarian, gave Dick ether, opened Dick up, got the poker out and sewed him up again. He tells me he's as good as ever, and I'm going down today to get him."

Making certain that the facts in the lead are correct and that the construction is right constitute more than half the task of copy editing. In the case of the direct news lead, the questions who or what, where, when and why or how, must be answered. If the location of the news event is the most striking, it must come first; if the "who" or "what" is the news point, the lead must be shaped so that that fact is the most prominently displayed. Every opening word is important. The word "the" should be used as little as possible in beginning a story, but it is not necessary to strain language or torture sentence structure to avoid it. To prevent using the word "the" as the opening word of a story, the participial clause was invented; but the method has been much abused.

An example of the "who" lead follows:

CAIRO, Oct. 6—President Anwar el-Sadat of Egypt was shot and killed today by a group of men in military uniform who hurled hand grenades and fired rifles at him as he watched a military parade commemorating the 1973 war against Israel.

The following illustrates the "what" lead:

LISBURN, Northern Ireland, Oct. 1—The British Army's role in maintaining order in Northern Ireland has decreased significantly both in the numbers involved and in the missions assigned, while the Royal Ulster Constabulary has assumed increased responsibility for security.

Here is a "where" lead:

LONDON, July 12—London and other British cities hit by nine days of rioting appeared generally calm today as heavy police reinforcements managed to contain sporadic outbreaks of vandalism by roaming youth gangs.

This is a "why" or "how" lead:

WASHINGTON, April 29—The United States ended two decades of military involvement in Vietnam today with the evacuation of about 1,000 Americans and more than 5,000 South Vietnamese from Saigon.

The "when" lead is illustrated in the following:

WASHINGTON, Aug. 8—On his 2,027th and penultimate day as President of the United States, with his staff and family unable to conceal their anguish, Richard M. Nixon went composedly through the schedule of a busy President.

If it is necessary to give authority to the story, the responsibility should be fixed at once. If the person making a statement is important, that is a vital point in the story and his name should appear as quickly as possible. Often a story is a story merely on account of the person or persons involved in it. A good rule for the copy editor is to let every man assume responsibility for his own statements or actions. It is not necessary for the newspaper to do so.

Here is illustrated the wrong way to write a story, in which responsibility should have been fixed at once and the authority cited:

The city's policy toward relief for the unemployed was condemned as "political" and as seeking to use public money to strengthen the hold of one party on the voters at a luncheon yesterday of the Southside Chamber of Commerce. After a strong plea had been made for an inquiry into the distribution and use of the $3,000,000 fund to aid the destitute through the winter, a resolution was adopted demanding that the Mayor instruct the City Controller to investigate immediately and to report promptly.

The attack was made by James A. Osgood, banker, who was the chairman of the campaign to raise private funds to supply jobs to 10,000 heads of families. He has long been an intimate friend of the Mayor and has previously supported the city's activities to relieve distress.

The following illustrates the proper method:

James A. Osgood, banker, who was chairman of the campaign to raise private funds to supply jobs to 10,000 heads of families, and who has long been an intimate friend of the Mayor, condemned yesterday the city's policy toward relief for the unemployed as "political" and as seeking to use public money to strengthen the hold of one party on the voters. The attack was made at a luncheon of the Southside Chamber of Commerce.

After Mr. Osgood had made a strong plea for an inquiry into the distribution and use of the $3,000,000 fund to aid the destitute through the winter, the Chamber adopted a resolution demanding that the Mayor instruct the City Controller to investigate immediately and to report promptly.

A point to be remembered about leads is that the lead is not always restricted to one sentence and may be more than one paragraph.

THE DEVELOPMENT

When the lead is satisfactory, the development of the rest of the story is comparatively simple. The reporter or copy editor should make sure that the narrative, exposition or description develops logically or naturally. In the case of the direct news lead, in which the story is summarized or the main point emphasized, a common practice is to return at once to the time when the story naturally starts and tell the events in the order in which they happened. Another method is to relate the occurrences in the order of their importance, rather than in sequence, but it requires more ingenuity to insure a smooth development. Skill in transition is required to avoid a jerky effect.

The "sequence" method of developing a news story after the lead is illustrated thus:

Surprised and overpowered by hold-up men they had been sent to capture, two detectives of the Second Avenue Station faced departmental charges last night because they had allowed themselves to be robbed of their revolvers and bound with other victims at Second Avenue and Third Street.

A robbery there Monday night, carried out with more than 60 policemen in the vicinity, was kept secret by the police until yesterday morning. Then it became known that three gunmen had escaped from the offices of the XYZ Company with $2,000 and that the two policemen who had started out in the role of captors had become captives.

One of the men was Detective A. B. Jones, a veteran of the force, and the other was Detective R. A. Smith, who has been commended for arresting armed robbers.

At about 10 o'clock Monday night, according to F. O. Adams, manager of the company, he had taken the day's receipts of $2,000 from the safe, placed them in his pocket and was preparing to go home when three men entered. When he attempted to fight them one intruder struck Adams three times on the head with the butt of a pistol. Once inside, each of them drew a second pistol and rounded up two drivers who were on the premises.

Adams did not know that detectives had been called but he learned later that the thieves had failed to notice the presence of a night watchman, who telephoned for the police.

The robbers searched Adams, found the $2,000 and then ordered him to open the safe. Then a knock sounded on the door.

"One of the robbers opened the door and said, 'Come right in gentlemen,'" said Adams. "Smith came in first and Jones right after him. Neither one had his revolver drawn. Then the robbers ordered the detectives . . ."

In this example the development of the story begins with the phrase "at about 10 o'clock Monday night" and continues chronologically to give the details.

The development of facts in the order of their importance is more difficult, as this illustration shows:

[1] WASHINGTON, March 31—First hearings on the President's Federal securities measure went swiftly forward today in House and Senate committees, developing some difference of opinion and bringing out testimony that of $50,000,000,000 in securities floated in this country in the last thirteen years half had proved either "worthless or undesirable."

[2] Chairman X of the Interstate and Foreign Commerce Committee of the House, in which lengthy testimony was taken today, said that hearings would end Monday noon at the latest and possibly tomorrow.

[3] The Senate Banking and Currency Committee, which held a short hearing today, indicated that it would await action by the House, which is expected to come not later than the middle of next week.

[4] The conflict of opinion arose among Congressional leaders over just what securities the pending act would apply to. Senator Y, the Democratic leader, said that "if you don't apply the law to existing securities you lose 90 percent of the value of the law," and it was his opinion that the measure would be made to apply to all outstanding issues.

[5] This was in sharp disagreement, however, with the views of the authors of the measure, including a former chairman of the Federal Trade Commission, and a representative of the Attorney General.

[6] They told the House committee that the law could apply only to flotations hereafter made or to securities which have already been authorized but not advertised or offered for sale to the public before the effective date of the new act.

[7] House Democratic leaders are preparing to make a determined stand for the securities measure, this determination being strengthened by intimations that some classes of issues would seek to have themselves exempted from the "pitiless publicity" requirements of the measure.

[8] While they laid plans for swift action on the first step of the President's permanent program of protection for investors and de-

positors, the two other steps, to establish better supervision of the
stock and commodity exchanges and eliminate unethical and unsafe
banking practices, continued in abeyance pending action on the securities bill.

[9] Informal consideration of these subjects was going forward,
however, both in official and business circles. A special committee
of the Chamber of Commerce of the United States recommended
in a report a single, unified commercial banking system for the country. The report suggested that every commercial bank, as distinguished from an investment institution, should ultimately be part of
the Federal Reserve System.

[10] Sponsors of the securities act had not been informed tonight
how many types of security issuers would seek to avoid its provisions.
It was reported that railroad companies would oppose vigorously their
inclusion in the part of the measures which compels detailed information about the issuer in any advertisement of a security flotation.

[11] An appeal was made openly to the House Committee to ex-
empt building and loan associations from the requirement for registration of every security issue. This plea was made on the basis that
such registration would work great inconvenience to many mutual
building and loan societies, while the fee would work financial hard-
ship.

[12] The railroad companies are not included among the issuers
required by the act to register detailed information with the Federal
Trade Commission, since their securities must be passed upon under
present law by the Interstate Commerce Commission.

[13] But the exemptions to railroad companies are not repeated
under the section providing for information that must be set forth
if a stock issue is advertised to the public.

[14] Under that provision the railroads, if they advertised a stock
or bond issue or if one were advertised for them by an investment
house, would have to set forth an account of the whole transaction,
including the fees to be paid to the bankers for handling the loan,
the name of the underwriting syndicate, the capital structure of the
railroad, including its assets and liabilities, and its profits and losses
during the year just preceding the offering.

[15] Representative Z of New York, former chairman of the commerce committee and an authority on the railroad problem, insisted
that jurisdiction over flotations of the carrier companies should be
left entirely to the Interstate Commerce Commission, as at present.

[16] The House committee spent the greater part of the day lis-

tening to an explanation of the bill by the former chairman of the F.T.C., who took it up section by section, giving the history and the purpose of each and discussing with members the feasibility or desirability of changes here and there in the text.

[17] Out of it all came the clear indication that the framers of the measure as well as the Democrats of the committee proposed to stand by it practically as written. They had already concluded that the bill was virtually "airtight."

[18] Questions from the Republican side left an inference that an attempt would be made to make the bill more specific as to the control of the Federal Trade Commission over the floatation of foreign securities in the United States.

[19] Under the terms of the bill the American underwriting syndicate or agent of a foreign government or industrial enterprise is compelled to register any proposed issue along with the information required. The only veto power the commission would have would be to revoke the registration and thus outlaw the issue.

[20] Representative XY of New Jersey insisted that the commission should have authority to stop foreign flotations without subterfuge.

[21] The witness answered that blunt action of that nature might offend sensitive governments to the point that they would construe it as an unfriendly act. He related that the State Department had practically such authority all along but hesitated to use it on that account.

[22] The chief of the Foreign Service Division of the Department of Commerce said that the State Department had been "very reluctant" to concern itself with foreign stock issues because of the lack of specific law on the subject. He said that under the pending act the Federal Trade Commission could discuss any particular foreign issue with the Cabinet officers involved and with representatives of the foreign power, and, on the basis of facts developed, ask the borrowing government to withdraw its issue if undesirable or of doubtful worth.

[23] "If the government in question should persist in its offering and refuse to withdraw its security issue, then the Federal Trade Commission could revoke its registration and no offense legitimately could be taken," he said.

[24] Under questioning of Mr. XY, he estimated that $12,000,000,000 in foreign securities, both governmental and private, had been issued in this country. He declined to estimate how many had gone into default, saying simply that a "very substantial portion" had either "gone bad" or deteriorated to the point of worthlessness.

[25] He was also authority for the estimate that $50,000,000,000 in securities had been floated in the United States in thirteen years, and that about half of them proved undesirable or worthless.

[26] "This law is designed to stop that sort of business," he said.

[27] The former F.T.C. chairman explained in his testimony that the bill was based on the theory that adequate public information about security issues would amply protect the public.

[28] "We can't protect fools," he said, "but we can give investors every reasonable opportunity to obtain information through the Federal Trade Commission on securities offered for sale."

[29] He referred frequently to the British securities act, from which many of the bill's ideas were taken, and to the Martin act of New York State, from which the language was copied.

[30] He also referred often to a copy of the book of Associate Justice Brandeis of the Supreme Court on "Other People's Money."

[31] A model advertisement for stock issues under the proposed law was lifted bodily from this book and placed in the record.

[32] The Attorney General's representative declared that the bill's purpose could be summed up in the words: "Pitiless publicity of all facts of which purchasers of securities should be informed."

This story merits the close reading and analyis of the student of journalism. Not only is a long and complicated story well developed as to the lead and subsequent structure, but it also shows excellent condensation of the mass of testimony taken before the House committee. It will be noted that the first three paragraphs constitute the lead, stating the highlights of the story—that hearings went forward swiftly on the securities measure, that differences of opinion developed, that testimony was given that half the huge total of securities floated in this country in thirteen years was of doubtful value—and making clear the status of the bill in Congress. The development of the story begins with paragraph 4 with the transition words "the conflict of opinion arose" which, reiterating a phrase in paragraph 1 in almost identical words, shows that that phrase of the lead is to be dealt with. Paragraphs 5 and 6 elaborate this, each paragraph developing smoothly from the preceding

one because of the transition words "this was in sharp disagreement" and "they told the House committee." Paragraph
7 introduces two new subjects—the Democratic leaders' attitude and the demand for exemptions from the provisions of
the bill—which can be expected to come up again later in
detail.

Paragraph 8 brings in still another subject that is almost
parenthetical—the status of other bills relating to the same
situation—but it is done smoothly with the clause "while they
laid plans for swift action." Paragraph 9 elaborates paragraph
8 and that phase of the story is then completed.

Paragraph 10 begins the development of the "exemption
phase" of the story, first stated in paragraph 7, and is also
elaboration of the lead point of "difference of opinion." Paragraphs 11, 12, 13, 14 and 15 continue and complete this
subject. Paragraph 16 gives in detail the hearing before the
House committee, one of the lead points, and recurs to paragraph 5 where the former F.T.C. chairman is mentioned as
a witness. Paragraph 17, worked in smoothly with the clause
"out of it all came the clear indication," elaborates and explains
paragraph 7. Paragraph 18, elaborated in paragraphs 19, 20
and 21, refers inferentially to the lead point concerning worthless securities, a phase of the story that is given in full detail
in paragraphs 22, 23, 24, 25, and 26. The former trade commission official's testimony is dealt with in paragraphs 27, 28,
29, 30 and 31. Paragraph 32 touches on the testimony of the
Attorney General's aide, mentioned specifically in paragraph
5.

To recapitulate briefly, three points were stated in the lead,
necessitating their elaboration and substantiation in the development in the order of importance. The difference of opinion was dealt with first, then the detail of the hearing bringing

out various phases of the differences, and then the testimony concerning worthless securities. It is beside the point whether there is agreement on this order of news values; the writer so rated them and developed his story accordingly. It may be of interest to note that the headline for this story was "Securities Hearing Divides Leaders; Measure Is Rushed."

While transition sentences or phrases are less common in newspaper writing than elsewhere, they preserve the unity of the story. This is particularly true, as in the foregoing case, when one point in the lead has been amplified and another is to be taken up.·Transition phrases frequently seen are "earlier in the day," "just before his arrival" and "prior to this development." The word "meanwhile" or the phrase "in the meantime" serve also for transition when the story turns to events that happened simultaneously with those previously related.

In the lead, the striking points have been summarized only. In the development, these points must be amplified but not repeated as matters of new fact. If the copy editor discovers that they are not mentioned again, there is something wrong with the development, or the inclusion of those points in the lead is questionable. Every fact in the lead must be supported later in detail; or it must be dealt with to the extent of giving enough background facts to show why it is important.

Such a case as this occurs often. A man mentioned as a candidate for office may, in the course of an otherwise routine speech, indicate that he will enter the contest or that he will not. This fact alone makes a story and is, of course, the lead. But the bald statement cannot stand alone. The background must be told by the reporter or supplied by a rewrite man or the copy editor to show the significance of the action. The statement is lifted from its context to construct the news story properly, but substance must be given to it by showing why it is important.

In modern journalism it is no longer felt that the five W's must be set forth at once or completely. In the interest of clear and simple writing it is now considered better to state the main point tersely, readably and forcefully, letting the contributory facts follow in a natural development of the story. This is a step in the direction of informing the reader faster. To insure his attention and comprehension, one idea to one sentence is regarded as essential. And the shorter the sentence the better.

Involved also is the need to give background and essential interpretation to inform the reader fully. This new element of reporting deserves some discussion. Fundamentally, a fact is a physical thing—a fire, an automobile crash, a speech, a convention—which are events that can be recorded in a straightforward account.

But consider the instance of Senator Jones, a member of the Senate Foreign Relations Committee, who makes a speech on the floor of the Senate giving his views of the current crisis and his proposals for meeting it. The only facts are that he spoke and that he made proposals which will be quoted at the necessary length and the text printed if warranted by his importance and the nature of his solution. This would meet the old, and largely continuing, formula of news writing.

Is this enough? The crisis Senator Jones is dealing with might be a crucial episode in United States relations with a foreign power and to report only his remarks might leave the reader in the dark. He is not fully informed and certainly not enlightened.

The speech must be set in a background of the whole complex picture of foreign relations at the moment, the position of this and other countries, how their policies can be affected by the views of this important official, what Washington reaction and that of other capitals is or might be.

To meet current requirements of news writing, it probably would be necessary to employ the time-honored "informed sources," "a spokesman," "observers," "persons close to the Secretary" and the like.

There is a danger here to the accepted principle that news should be gathered and published objectively. There is a thin line between interpretation and opinion. Great skill in phrasing is required to add perspective and depth to a set of facts without expressing or indicating a point of view.

Nevertheless these goals—simplicity, clarity, depth and perspective—are increasingly needed as local, national and foreign situations become more complex. There is a growing need also to inform newspaper readers quickly because of the keen competition for a share of their leisure time.

THE SENTENCE

The short simple sentence is the most effective for news writing. As in every other kind of writing, however, there must be variety. A common misconception among beginners is that the first sentence must contain the answers to the questions who or what, where, when and why or how. This leads invariably to an involved sentence structure that is neither clear nor effective. The copy editor should break up long sentences, even though they may be clear. The effect of a sentence is lost if a dozen lines of type must be read before the end is reached.

The involved one-sentence lead is illustrated thus:

Returning to the city yesterday from a two-week vacation in the South, Governor Anderson issued a statement of defiance to his opponents, who, according to reports in political circles, are planning to "put him in a hole" over the tax measure that is expected to be drafted next week at a meeting of the Republican leaders, by throwing upon the executive the burden of seeking new sources of revenue and forcing the executive to shoulder the political consequences of what may prove to be an unpopular program, and declared that he was ready for a fight to the finish on the legislative measures that he considered to be of paramount importance at this session.

A better way to write the lead is:

Returning to the city yesterday from a two-week vacation in the South, Governor Anderson issued a statement of defiance to his opponents and declared that he was ready for a fight to the finish on the legislative measures that he considered to be of paramount importance at this session.

The Republicans, according to reports in political circles, are planning to "put him in a hole" over the tax measure that is expected to be drafted next week at a meeting of the Republican leaders. They plan to throw upon the governor the burden of seeking new sources of revenue and force him to shoulder the political consequences of what may prove to be an unpopular program.

Paragraphing is not haphazard and usually not an arbitrary breaking up of the story into units for regular type display. Paragraphing, like sentence structure, must follow the rules of rhetoric. For an extended discussion, grammar books should be consulted. In general, a paragraph indicates to the reader that a new subject or a new phase of the same subject is to be taken up. Everything relating to the same phase of the news story should, if possible, be in the same paragraph, although long paragraphs are as much to be avoided as long sentences.

For emphasis a separate paragraph may be made arbitrarily, and direct quotations usually should be paragraphed.

The following is an example of bad paragraphing:

A clamor over opening the road began when the state took control of it on completion of the pipeline in 1977.

Sportsmen wanted access to remote fishing and hunting areas.

Business interests thought opening it might help the states economy.

Miners wanted to get to their claims. But truckers believed tourists would create traffic hazards.

Indians and Eskimos wanted to keep people out of their hunting areas, believing that whites who shoot for trophies and not for the meat would deplete the game.

Safety conscious officials worried about tourists coming onto the highway, unfamiliar with the country and ill-equipped to look after themselves.

"I resisted it being thrown wide open," said Gov. Jay Hammond. "I wanted it opened in stages."

That was what a Superior Court judge in Fairbanks ordered done in late winter.

If paragraphed in the following manner, the unity of thought is retained:

A clamor over opening the road began when the state took control of it on completion of the pipeline in 1977. Sportsmen wanted access to remote fishing and hunting areas. Business interests thought opening it might help the state's economy. Miners wanted to get to their claims.

But truckers believed tourists would create traffic hazards. Indians and Eskimos wanted to keep people out of their hunting areas, believing that whites who shoot for trophies and not for the meat would deplete the game. Safety-conscious officials worried about tourists coming onto the highway, unfamiliar with the country and ill-equipped to look after themselves.

"I resisted it being thrown wide open," said Gov. Jay Hammond. "I wanted it opened in stages." That was what a Superior Court judge in Fairbanks ordered done in late winter.

TONING DOWN AND BRIGHTENING UP

The copy editor frequently hears the order, "tone it down." This means that the story has been phrased too strongly or that the perspective is wrong. Often the toning-down process can be accomplished merely by eliminating adjectives, changing strong verbs to milder ones and striking out words that characterize or describe in a manner that is distasteful. The order "clean it up" has a similar intent, but refers usually to crime or similar stories that are told in too explicit language. Good taste often is involved and it is the copy editor's task to eliminate offensive phases of the story. This kind of editing does not entail the suppression of facts; it merely requires that the story be told in polite language.

Here is a story that should be toned down:

JERSEY CITY, N.J., Jan. 12—Several neighbors saw Gustaf A. Petersen in his backyard at 101 Twenty-fifth Street, Union City, today sharpening a knife on a whetstone. At intervals Petersen stopped to examine the knife, which had a six-inch blade and was of a type used by shoemakers.

Mrs. William Orr, whose kitchen window looks out over Petersen's yard, saw him examine the knife for the fourth or fifth time. Then, she told the police, she saw him smile as if pleased, raise the knife and slash his throat. She shouted for help. Several men climbed over fences to reach Petersen. He was taken to the North Hudson Hospital in Weehawken but he was dead on arrival there.

Petersen was 51 years old and was a ship's carpenter.

The story may be edited as follows to remove the gruesome features:

JERSEY CITY, N.J., Jan. 12—Gustaf A. Petersen, 51 years old, a ship's carpenter, committed suicide in his backyard at 101 Twenty-fifth Street, Union City, today by slashing his throat with a knife. Mrs. William Orr, whose kitchen window overlooks Petersen's yard, saw his act and summoned help. Several neighbors told the police that they had seen Petersen in his yard whetting the knife, which had a six-inch blade and was of the type used by shoemakers.

"Brightening up" a story requires the judicious use of adjectives or of colorful or active verbs, or the "lifting" of a phrase or sentence from the detail of the story to the lead, helping to transform the whole from a dull account into an interesting one.

Examine the following statistical story to see what can be done with it to make it of interest to readers.

OSSINING, N.Y., Jan. 3—Sing Sing authorities disclosed today that a total of 1,740 lawbreakers were received at the prison last year, 1,038 were transferred by the warden to upstate prisons and that the prison population at the end of the year was more than 2,400.

Besides those tranferred the total number of convicts was reduced by 555, 32 of whom died and 523 of whom were discharged. Four hundred and eighty were paroled; 10 were pardoned by the Governor: 9 won reversals of their convictions; certificates of reasonable doubt were granted to 2 and 14 were released for resentencing. Only 8 of those discharged from the prison served their maximum terms.

It probably will be agreed that only one fact strikes the eye as being of general interest and that the last one: that "only eight served their maximum terms." The problem then is to make that fact the lead. It appears to be a rewrite man's work, but it can be edited by clipping the story in two between the paragraphs, writing a paragraph lead, editing the second paragraph to read smoothly from the new lead and editing the old lead to go at the end. This is how it will look:

OSSINING, N.Y., Jan. 3—Only eight of 523 prisoners discharged from Sing Sing prison this year served their maximum terms, it was disclosed at the prison today.

The total number of convicts was reduced by 32 deaths. Of the 523 discharged, 480 were paroled; 10 were pardoned by the Governor; 9 won reversals of their convictions; certificates of reasonable doubt were granted to 2 and 14 were released for resentencing.

During the year 1,740 lawbreakers were received at the prison and 1,038 were transferred by the warden to upstate prisons. The prison population at the end of the year was more than 2,400.

TRIMMING, CUTTING, AND BOILING DOWN

The copy editor frequently must shorten a story to fit into a space indicated, or to enable the editor in charge to keep within his total space allotment. This entails trimming, cutting, and boiling down, which are similar processes but which vary in degree.

Trimming is a general tightening up of the story, chiefly by eliminating superfluous words and replacing loose phrases with single words that express the thought adequately. The following is an example of paragraphs that should be trimmed:

The Governor, upon whom the duty of finding the necessary funds to keep the state machinery moving devolves, will deal in detail with the measures which he has formulated with this end in view, when his executive budget is presented to the law-making body next week. He has given little or no intimation as to what measure he will recommend to provide the necessary funds. It is the prevailing opinion among persons in his confidence, however, that he will resort to no new forms of taxation but will depend on increasing existing levies. It appears to be definitely known, however, by friends of the Governor that doubling of the present tax on gasoline will be asked.

While the Governor declared entirely unfounded reports that the state treasury was nearly empty, he admitted that resort to short term borrowing might be necessary in order to provide funds for the administrative departments.

The Assembly Republicans met in caucus tonight for the purpose of designating their leaders.

Trimming will reduce these 163 words to 116, a saving of 47 words, or one-fourth of the space, thus:

The Governor, who must find the necessary funds to keep the state machinery moving, will deal in detail with revenue measures when his executive budget is presented next week. He has given little intimation what measure he will recommend. It is the opinion of persons in his confidence, however, that he will resort to no new forms of taxation but will depend on increasing existing levies. It appears definite that doubling of the tax on gasoline will be asked.

The Governor denied reports that the state treasury was nearly empty, but admitted short term borrowing might be necessary to provide funds for the administrative departments.

The Assembly Republicans met in caucus tonight to designate their leaders.

Two phrases should be noted: "in order to," which can nearly always be shortened to "to"; and "for the purpose of," which also usually can be expressed simply by "to."

Boiling down is more drastic and is the process of close paring of all sentences and the sacrifice of minor facts. Here is a problem in boiling down:

Several lame and elderly subway passengers, frightened by the lightning-like flashes of a short circuit, had to be assisted last night from the BMT tracks under Seventh Avenue to the street near Forty-ninth Street by an emergency exit, followed by 200 other passengers, in an accident that caused a traffic tie-up for twenty minutes. No one was injured.

The mishap occurred at 7:55 P.M. when a Brighton local train, headed north for Queens Plaza, was approaching the Forty-ninth Street station. A piece of equipment beneath one car came in contact with the third rail, causing the short circuit.

The train had sufficient momentum to carry it into the Forty-ninth Street station, where the engineer halted it to allow the passengers to be discharged. Soon after the train stopped, a northbound Fourth Avenue local approached on the same tracks. The engineer of this train, seeing the Brighton local in the station, stopped his train short of the station platform. The vivid electric flashes, lighting up the tunnel, frightened some of the passengers of the Fourth Avenue local. In a few moments, however, the power was shut off, leaving the train stranded several hundred feet from the Forty-ninth Street station platform.

With the danger of the deadly third rail removed, the passengers on the crowded train were allowed to leave the cars. They scrambled to the tracks, picked their way through the darkness to the emergency exit, helping the more timid passengers as they went.

During the twenty minutes in which the power was off all northbound local trains on the line were rerouted along the center tracks which run from Times Square and are used ordinarily for the shunting of express trains which end their runs at the Square.

Boiling down reduces the number of words from 285 to 165, a saving of 120 words, or two-fifth of the space formerly required, as follows:

Several lame and elderly subway passengers, frightened by the flashes of a short circuit caused when a piece of equipment struck the third rail, had to be assisted last night from the BMT tracks under Seventh Avenue to the street near Forty-ninth Street by an emergency exit, followed by 200 other passengers. The accident tied up traffic for twenty minutes. No one was injured.

The mishap occurred at 7:55 P.M. when a northbound Brighton local was approaching the Forty-ninth Street station. It had sufficient momentum to carry it into the station, where the passengers were discharged.

Soon afterward, a Fourth Avenue local approached on the same tracks. The engineer stopped his train short of the station. The vivid electric flashes frightened some passengers but soon the power was shut off, leaving the train stranded. With the danger of the third rail removed, the passengers were allowed to leave the cars to grope through darkness to the exit.

While the power was off all northbound local trains were rerouted.

Cutting means the elimination of all but the most important facts, those without which there would be no story or an incomplete one. Often there is nothing left but the bare bones of a story with a shred or two of clothing. Many news stories can be so reduced without loss to the reader. Routine court stories, which must be published for one reason or another, can be cut to brief, unadorned recitals.

Here is a story to be cut:

New Yorkers are so accustomed to shouting at one another above the crash of steel and stone, the din of subways and noise of traffic that they shout over the dinner table in voices that are not musical but piercing and strident, Jack Robinson, the writer, told a radio audience yesterday afternoon over Station XYZ.

Mr. Robinson complained that even the exterior walls of buildings are sound boxes which hurl back noises into suffering ears, and as a remedy he suggested the use of acoustically treated surfacing.

Speaking under the auspices of the New York Noise Abatement Commission, Mr. Robinson told his listeners that the most offensive noises originate with such transit facilities as subway trains, brake-screeching automobiles and horn-honking taxicabs. A group of persons in a European restaurant and a group from a similar social background in a New York eating place, he went on, form a remarkable contrast.

"In Europe," he said, "the conversation is subdued, yet far more audible because it is more musical than with us. You can't expect the New Yorker to bring his voice down again during the lunch or dinner hour if all the rest of the day he must compete with the crash of steel and stone around him."

He added that our descendents will no doubt marvel that "we put up with the torture of riveting machines which are building a house next door, but will marvel much more that we endured so long without protest noises which were not temporary but part of our life from year's end to year's end."

When cut, this story looks like this:

New Yorkers are so accustomed to shouting at one another above the city's clamor that they shout over the dinner table in piercing and strident voices, Jack Robinson, the writer, told a radio audience yesterday afternoon over Station XYZ. He spoke under the auspices of the New York Noise Abatement Commission.

Mr. Robinson complained that even the exterior walls of buildings are sound boxes which hurl back noises and suggested the use of acoustically treated surfacing. He said that the more offensive noises originate with subways, automobiles, trucks, and taxicabs. Our descendants, he said, will marvel that we endured such din so long.

The voices of Europeans, he added, are musical and, while subdued, more audible.

By this method the story of 264 words has been reduced to 116 or to less than half. This drastic treatment depends wholly upon the space allotted to the story and is resorted to only in cases where the press of news is so great that much must be lost.

FAIRNESS, PUBLICITY, AND LIBEL

In any of these processes, care should be taken that no elimination of a fact leaves a wrong impression. Both sides to a dispute or lawsuit should have equal treatment. If the removal of a fact distorts the story in any respect, if a question is left in the mind, the fact should be retained.

As to fairness, the copy editor should make sure that every party to a controversy gets a hearing. If a man is accused, an effort should be made to include his comment in the same story in which the charges are published. Sometimes this effort is indicated only by a sentence saying that the accused man "could not be reached for comment." This tends to show the impartiality of the newspaper. If no effort to obtain both sides of the story has been made, the copy editor should call the attention of the editor in charge to the failure to do so.

While trimming, cutting or boiling down, the copy editor should take special pains to remove words or names that give unwarranted publicity to persons or things, or that tend to advertise improperly stores or other places or goods of any kind.

He should also eliminate editorial opinion or any bias that tends, or might tend, to indicate an attitude or opinion by the newspaper or the copy editor himself. Some freedom is allowed in news stories that are written under a byline, that is, signed by the writer, but this leeway is limited by the policy of the newspaper. For example, a political writer is permitted in a signed story to express, usually in a highly qualified manner, his views of the outcome of a campaign.

Libel is generally described as the publication of material that impeaches the honesty, integrity, virtue or reputation of a living person, thereby holding him up to public ridicule or contempt or causing him financial injury. It is not always possible to avoid printing some libelous statements, but if the newspaper is sued for damages, its defenses are four: (1) to prove that the defamatory statements were true; (2) to show that the statements were part of a court record or other official or public proceedings and therefore privileged; (3) to show that the publication was in good faith and without malice (this is not strictly a defense, but a plea in mitigation of damages); (4) to show that the person involved is a public official or a public figure.

The copy editor should remember that such phrases as "it was said," "it was alleged," and "according to the police," are no protection against a libel suit, but they tend to show a lack of malice and are therefore valuable. The questions "Is it true?" and "Is it privileged?" serve as a general rule of thumb that will solve many problems of the copy editor. He should, however, become familiar with the libel laws of his state and have more than a slight acquaintance with case histories.

The copy editor should be careful to avoid anonymous or irresponsible statements. He should beware also of the "funny stories" lest the persons named or indicated be made to appear ridiculous.

When the copy editor is in doubt about a point in a story, four courses are open to him. If the questioned fact is not vital, it may be deleted. This should be a last resort, however, not an easy way out of a difficulty. If the question can be cleared up by means of a reference book, it should be checked in that manner. If it can be checked only by reference to the reporter, he should be consulted. Questions of policy, taste or consistency usually are referred to the head of the desk for decision, and by him to higher editors if it becomes necessary.

SUBHEADS

Stories of more than half a column in length are broken up by subheads. These are, in effect, small one-line headlines and should follow the rules for headlines; that is, to say something, not to be merely labels. They are set in body type but have a blacker face. They should be placed about every quarter-column, but there should rarely be fewer than two. Practice varies as to where they should be placed, some newspapers requiring that they be inserted regularly for balance, and others requiring that they be placed at the natural "breaks" in the subject matter of the story.

The purpose of subheads is to interrupt long stretches of type that are unattractive to the reader's eye and to indicate the subject matter of the type appearing under them.

HEADLINES

When the copy has been edited with attention to the foregoing suggestions, the copy editor's next task is to write a headline for the story. The headline, which is fully considered in the second part of this book, must first be accurate, not only in point of fact but also in spirit. Facts can be so placed in reference to one another that a meaning apart from the words themselves may be derived. The headline also should tell the whole story, or as much of it as space will permit, in a forceful and attractive way.

It has been noted that students of journalism concentrate on headline writing more than on the editing of copy. This is perhaps owing to the fact that headline writing is a challenge to their ingenuity and that headlines show to better advantage than editing. No error could be graver. If such a point of view carries over into the newspaper work, the copy editor will be disillusioned speedily.

4. ELECTRONIC EDITING

EARLY in the 1970's, the electronic industry devised and perfected computer-operated systems that revolutionized newspaper publishing. A business that had thrived for nearly 100 years on the performance of the linotype machine in producing newspapers had come on hard times and was slowly dying because of enormous production costs, largely for labor in the composing and proofrooms. The largest papers required hundreds of skilled workers in each of these departments, and in the composing room it also needed hundreds of costly linotype machines.

In this period there were long months of negotiations between publishers and Big Six, the printer's union in New York, over automation, or the use of computerized tape to set newspaper type. The union resorted for months to delays and harassing tactics and in the end agreed to an eleven-year contract that opened the way to the all-important tape, the retraining of many of their members for other jobs in the field and the orderly retirement of many of the older members. The sole aim of the publishers was to meet the union's demands and insure the approval of automation.

It was a costly settlement for the publishers and it has some years yet to run but it guaranteed a brighter future in which newspapers could exist, and profitably. It killed the linotype machine and thereby also the expensive composing rooms and proofrooms and ended the need for large manpower pools in both of them. Gone also were the myriad union rules that labor had set up to fatten its paycheck and limit the initiative of the owners.

Out of this welter of invention and negotiations came an answer to the replacement of the linotype operator and the proofreader. When and how are not in the record but the key was obviously the nature of electronic computation itself. To set type by electronic tape required a terminal keyboard, like a typewriter's, and an operator with information or news to put on that tape. This made the newspaper reporter the natural candidate for the job.

All that had to be done was to retrain him to use a computer terminal keyboard. This was simple, since the reporter has long used the similar typewriter keyboard and he could familiarize himself quickly with other keys and buttons on the computer device. These keys and buttons had latent powers that, when summoned, transformed them into the fantastic star performers of modern journalism.

The first step was for a reporter to learn how to enter the terminal to start a story, thus getting an identifying number for his story, and how to store the material or transfer it when he finished. Starting the story might be compared to putting paper in the typewriter, and storing or transferring it might be likened to the delivery of the paper to the desk or editor. When the terminal is turned on, the reporter can type away furiously and see all the words before him, but unless he has entered the terminal and gotten the identifying number, the words will have no permanence and will disappear as soon as the machine is turned off—sort of written on the light, rather than written on the wind.

Going beyond the basics enables the reporter to make use of all the capabilities of the computer system like transposing phrases or moving paragraphs or larger blocs of type.

One editor's comment on the uses and flexibility of the instrument was:

I would emphasize that the use of the computer terminal makes writing and editing immeasurably easier than on paper. There's no need to x-out mistakes and retype; inserts can be made without cutting and pasting or writing small between the lines. Reporters as well as editors can move words, sentences, paragraphs, or whole chunks of stories just by pressing a few buttons. . . . And after each change, the press of another button will give you an updated word count. Once a story is hyphenated and justified by the copy desk, the machine will measure its length in column inches.

At first glance it might appear that the reporter is the most affected by the electronic system, since he must master new mechanical procedures in a new medium to convert words and sentences (the news story) into electronic impulses and shape them into a cogent narration of an important or interesting event. But the fundamental rules of composing a news story are the same. The medium has changed, but not the method.

The copy editor also must be retrained in the use of the computer terminal, and in more detail, because he must edit the story along the general lines covered in the preceding sections and also according to a mass of style rules that may be applicable to his paper alone. These govern word usage, abbreviations, use of titles and whether they are spelled out or not, use of slang or idiom. For example there is great variation among publications in the use of Ms. for Miss or Mrs. and the use of Mr. after the full name has been given.

Both reporters and the copy desk must now be alert for detailed proofreading and correct any errors of fact, spelling, or grammar, and any violation of style rules of this publication. The final responsibility in this area is the copy editor's.

It might be well to stress here that a computer system is as good as its programming. It can turn out agate, 72-point headlines, indent stories for picture cut-ins, change typefaces and perform other magical functions at the pressing of the proper keys, but the computer will not tell you if the grammar is right, or if the spelling is correct or the facts accurate. Similarly, the computer will tell you if the headline fits, but it won't say whether it is a good head.

The great flood of news stories or information about them on any day or night in a newspaper office is kept track of by schedules or assignment sheets. Each department has one to show what each reporter is covering, and each department photostats its schedules and sends one or more to every other department. Each editor is thus kept aware of events in all areas. Schedules called directories are provided also by all wire services, and any story scheduled anywhere can be brought into the office by any computer terminal.

It may be useful to follow a metropolitan story through the electronic chain. The assignment editor of the metropolitan desk keeps an assignment sheet showing the reporters' names and the slugs of the stories each is covering. As each returns from the assignment, the reporter is asked to write a summary of the event covered, which is distributed to all chief editors and given a space allotment. The reporter's name and the assignment editor's slug identify the copy generally; the computer supplies the designation of numbers, which include the circuit or "system" used so that when the reporter "stores" the product to await editing, it can be called back from the memory bank. Most systems are protected by entry codes to prevent unauthorized use of the computer.

The reporter uses a keyboard on a computer terminal that contains the standard array of letters, numbers, punctuation, and symbols, but is also equipped with various electronic "command" keys that are used for all mechanical functions, such as spacing, corrections, insertions, deletions, transfer of words, sentences, or paragraphs, and justification of lines of type. The terminal also can be converted into a *dual or split screen* and thus call up two stories at once. This enables a reporter to have notes on one half of the screen while writing on the other, or to use another story as reference while one is being composed. Note that the use of the dual screen cuts down the number of lines that can be seen at one time. Thus on *New York Times* screens, the normal 26 lines is cut to 13 when dual screen is used.

Also, the dual column mode shows the story in two parts, which speeds the scrolling up and down time, enabling a writer or editor to check on what has gone before. Again, the number of lines is reduced when this mode is used.

By use of the *alternate cursor,* inserts can be transferred from one side of the screen to the other, allowing for the picking up of a long explanation from notes or reference material. The city or metropolitan desk and the local copy editors all are supplied with computer terminals just like the reporter's. As the editing process begins, the metropolitan editor or an assistant can recover each story from a memory bank for judgment as to its importance and its handling by the reporter. The story appears on the lighted screen and the editor makes any changes he wishes, all done electronically. If extensive revision is needed, the reporter is asked to revise the story and it is then restored to the memory bank to await detailed attention by the copy desk.

The head of the copy desk also works from a schedule of

This machine and other video display terminals like it have revolutionized the newspaper business, offering publishers an inexpensive and fast way for the work of reporters and editors to be turned into images that are converted by a computer and other machines into slick-paper printouts for paste-up in the photo offset process now used by major U.S. newspapers.

Reporter uses video display terminal (*top*) to compose story. Most computer systems using this type of equipment allow storing of material for further revision, cancellation of words and phrases rather than striking through, and calling up another story for reference by using the split-screen capability shown on the preceding page. Copy editors (*bottom*) edit stories on terminals, moving words, paragraphs or blocks of type around, correcting spelling and grammar, coding material for type size and column width, then sending the material to the composing room by the press of a button.

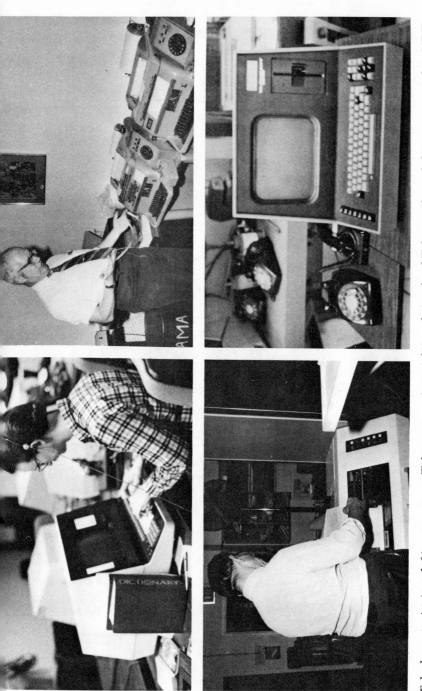

Telephone typist (*top left*) enters story. Teletype tape (*top right*) and signals of Teleram (*lower left*) are converted to VDT images by computer (*lower right*).

This is the modern computerized composing room, without a linotype machine in sight. The printers use the video display terminals shown to put editorial matter or advertising material into computer systems for editing or checking. The material is ultimately printed out on page forms that are then photographed for engraving plates that go on rotary presses.

Makeup man (*top*) reaches for printout of story sent to composing room by editors and converted into images on glossy paper by the photo machine. The machine has the capability of printing story and headline on the same sheet, ready for cutting to column size. After the reverse side of the glossy paper printout is coated with rubber cement, it is taken to page forms (*bottom*) and pasted in the proper place on the page by the makeup man under the guidance of the editor, with trims being made by the makeup man with a razor.

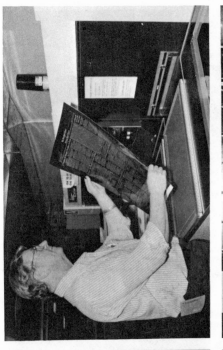

the stories produced by the reportorial staff. He assigns them to copy editors with proper consideration of each editor's ability and background for handling the story in hand. The copy editor calls up the assigned story to his computer screen by pressing the identifying code. He then edits the "copy," using the principles set out in detail in the preceding sections. These basic rules apply to computerized editing as they did to the "pencil and paste pot" method. The physical agency has been altered, but not the principles.

The copy editor also writes the specified headline, indicating the type required.

The completed product, now edited and proofread, is transmitted (by pressing the proper command key) to a printout section of the newsroom where a "hard copy" is made. This is used for reference by various editors who want visible manuscript or carbons at hand, a remnant of old-time practice.

At the same time the completed electronic product is sent to a photocomposing machine in the paste-up department, which produces columns of news material that are then cut and pasted into page formats, following schedules or page layouts furnished by makeup editors. These editors usually begin their work in the newsroom in close touch with the general editors but may move on to the paste-up area as the deadline nears.

These page formats are moved by electronic scanners to the press room, where they are projected onto thin metal plates in a machine that produces the printing surface of each newspaper page.

LOOKING AHEAD

Electronic production of newspapers is still in the trial and error period. There will be refinements in all areas, of course, but it appears safe to say that the general outline of procedures has been fairly well set.

Many publishers may have plunged into total electronic systems with the notion that no hard copy was necessary, which would represent a savings on paper and hardware. However, editors find that hard copy is essential for efficient operations, allowing for more than one viewing of the same story at one time, providing greater input from more sources and guarding against system failures at critical junctures.

There probably will have to be some rethinking of the decision to throw the main burden of electronics on the staff of reporters and copy editors. A new type of employee, part reporter, part mechanic, may be far in the newspapers' future. It may be that the new burdens on the reporter and the copy editors will be so onerous as to minimize drastically their value as fact gatherers and writers and as editors. Both groups have welcomed the computer system as an easier and more efficient way to accomplish their ends, but experience is likely to modify these opinions.

There is no doubt that publishers will move forward at once to standardize the computer terminal keyboard, of which there are a number of variations at present. They appear to favor on-the-job training at present, partly because of this variation, but a backlog of trained personnel soon will be required.

It would seem necessary for schools of journalism to take some steps now for this wave of the future and provide at least a skeleton set-up to train students. One element in such a course should be an introduction to the computer system, which could dispel many inaccuracies and improve confidence in it.

5. ABUSED WORDS

THE FOLLOWING lists of words, commonly misused by newspaper reporters and copy editors, has been compiled with the objects of helping to promote a discriminating use of English and of overcoming some of the stereotyped expressions found most frequently. It is an attempt to show by example how news copy can be made more expressive and direct and how clichés that survive by tradition in each generation of newspaper men can be eliminated. It is hoped that such a list will be of value in the newspaper office as well as to the student of journalism. It is necessarily a limited list. For extended discussion the reader is referred to *The Careful Writer* by Theodore M. Bernstein (Atheneum, 1965).

It should be kept in mind that preferred uses have been indicated for each word only in conjunction with the word coupled with it, and no attempt has been made to show proper uses in other senses.

This compilation is not designed to be exhaustive. It is not, and is not intended to be, a substitute for the dictionary; rather its use should stimulate attention to accurate definition and consequently bring about more discriminating use of words.

ACT—ACTION *The Governor's act in signing the bill was one step in the course of action he had outlined for public improvements.* An action may be composed on many acts.

ADMINISTER—DEAL *The blow was administered from behind* should read *The blow was dealt from behind.* However, *The Mayor ad-*

ministered the oath, The *physician administered the medicine* and
The President administered the affairs of the nation with success
are correct.

ADOPT—DECIDE UPON—ASSUME   *The Legislature adopted the resolution. He decided upon* (not adopted) *the course he had mapped out.
He assumed* (not adopted) *the role of burglar.*

AFFECT   *see* Effect

ALLEGE—SAY   *Alleged* is an overworked newspaper word. *Alleged
crime* is correct but *alleged criminal* is not, although the latter
expression may be condoned because it is the briefest way to express
the status of the incriminated person. Suspect or prisoner often
will serve for *alleged criminal. He said* (not alleged) *he was innocent,* but *He alleged his innocence.* Also, *He said* (not alleged) *that
he had flown to Greenland.*

ALL OF   The *of* is unnecessary. *The robber took all of the money* should
be *The robber took all the money.*

ALLUDE—REFER   The editor can determine only from the text of a
statement whether *allusion* or *reference* has been made. *He alluded
to strife in the party when he said, "We have had troubles enough."*
(Not mentioning directly.) *He referred to strife in the party when
he said, "Let us end this internal dissension."* (Mentioning directly.)

ALONE—ONLY   *The lawyer said that fright alone could have caused
the man's death* means that fright, without the aid of anything else,
could have caused the death. *The lawyer said that only fright could
have caused the man's death* means that nothing else than fright
could have done so.

ALTERNATIVE—CHOICE   *He had no choice* (not alternative) *but to flee.
These are the only choices* (not alternatives). *The alternatives were
to fight or to flee.*

AMATEUR—NOVICE   *The amateur's skill exceeded the professional
player's. The novice began his course of instruction at the age of
ten.*

AMONG—BETWEEN   *He distinguished between the two objects. He
must share it among five persons.* However, the relationship expressed by *among* is rather loose. When three or more things are
brought into a relationship severally and reciprocally, *between* is
proper. *Discussions between Washington, Cairo and Tel Aviv on
the Palestinian question were inconclusive.*

AND—TO   *Try and do it* is popular, but nevertheless is a vulgarism.
Try to do it is correct. *Come to* (not and) *see me. He planned to
go to the capital to see the Senator* does not mean the same thing
as *He planned to go to the capital and see the Senator.*

ANTICIPATE—EXPECT   *He anticipated the result and was prepared to try another plan. He expected no other result.*

ANXIOUS—EAGER   *He was anxious over the outcome of the election. He was eager* (not anxious) *to go.*

AS, AS—SO, AS   In affirmative comparisons *as, as* is correct, in negative *so, as. This is as good as that. This is not so good as that.*

AS IF   *As if* is better. *He looked as* (he would look) *though he were afraid* is illogical. *He looked as* (he would look) *if he were afraid* is correct.

ASSENT   *see* Consent

ASSUME   *see* Adopt

ATTORNEY   *see* Lawyer

AUDIENCE—SPECTATORS   An *audience* hears; *spectators* see.

AUTHENTIC   *see* Genuine

AVENGE   A person may *avenge* an injury with the idea of restoring a balance of justice and take *revenge* or *vengeance* out of a more personal resentment.

AVERAGE   *see* Mean

AVOID—AVERT   *The accident was averted when the captain avoided the reef.*

BALANCE—REMAINDER   *Balance* often is used indiscriminately for *remainder. His balance at the bank was five dollars. The remainder* (not balance) *of the day was wasted;* or better still, *The rest of the day was wasted.*

BEGIN, END—COMMENCE, COMPLETE   In almost all cases *begin* is preferable to *commence* in newspaper work. *Begin* and *end* are antonyms, as are *commence* and *complete.* A work of art is commenced and completed only when it has been perfected. A project may be begun and ended without being completed. *See also* Inaugurate.

BESIDE—BESIDES   *Beside* is always a preposition. *Besides* is both a preposition and an adverb. *He stood beside the table; Besides the book, he has the manuscript; Besides, he will not go.*

BETWEEN   *see* Among

BLAME IT ON   This is a colloquial expression. The verb form is *blame,* not blame on. *The accident happened at noon; it was blamed on the engineer.* How much better to say, *The accident happened at noon; the engineer was blamed.* It is better also to write *He said the tide caused the collision* than *He blamed the tide,* because only persons can be considered blameworthy.

BRAVERY—COURAGE   A policeman in a fight with robbers demonstrates his *bravery.* A timid man, having considered the dangers, shows *courage* in becoming a policeman.

BUT   *see* Else

BY—OF—WITH—FOR   *He was afflicted with* (not by) *rheumatism. He was distinguished for* (not by) *his learning.* However, *In comparison with that landscape, this picture is distinguished by its colors.*

CANINE—DOG   *Canine* does not mean a *dog. Canine* is the adjective, *dog* the noun.

CHOICE   *see* Alternative

CLAIM—SAY   *He claimed the property* is correct. *He claimed that he had been there* is improved by writing *He said that he had been there* or, if it is a matter of dispute, *He contended that he had been there. Claim a right* is correct but *assert a right* probably is preferable.

COMMENCE   *see* Begin

COMMONLY   *see* Generally

COMPARE WITH—COMPARE TO   *Lee's strategy in his campaigns can be compared to Napoleon's. He was compared with their former leader and found wanting in daring.*

COMPLETE   *see* Begin

CONCLUDE—END   Speeches, meetings and hearings are *closed* or *ended*, not *concluded. He concluded his argument and then went on to explain its implications.*

CONDEMN   *see* Criticize

CONSENT—ASSENT   *He consented to go to the conference but refused to assent to the interpretation of the treaty that representation must be limited.*

CONSIDER—THINK   *After long study, he said he considered the course unwise. He thinks the course is unwise. Think* does not necessarily exclude deliberation, but ordinarily is used in a more casual sense than consider.

CONTINUOUS—CONTINUAL   A succession of showers is *continual*; a steady downpour is *continuous.*

COURAGE   *See* Bravery

CRITICALLY—SERIOUSLY   *Critically* is frequently used when seriously or gravely express the intent better. *Critically ill* specifies a certain stage of the disease.

CRITICIZE—CONDEMN   *He criticized the book favorably. He condemned the book on the ground that it was propaganda.*

DEAL   *see* Administer

DECIDE UPON   *see* Adopt

DECISION   *see* Verdict

DIE OF   *One dies of disease* (not dies with, nor dies from, disease).

However, *one suffers from disease* (not with it) and is *afflicted with blindness* (not by it).

DIMENSIONS *see* Proportions

DISTRICT *see* Section

DOG *see* Canine

EAGER *see* Anxious

EARN *see* Make

EFFECT—AFFECT *The policeman effected the rescue at great risk to himself but he was not affected by his strenuous efforts.* The word *effect* is considerably overused in newspapers, however. *He effected the capture of the robbers quickly* would be improved by *He captured the robbers quickly.*

ELSE—BUT *Nothing else than* (not but) *repudiation will be accepted.* Or, *Nothing but repudiation will be accepted.*

END *see* Begin; Conclude

END RESULT *Result* is unnecessary. *The end.*

ENTAIL *see* Involve

ESSENTIAL—NECESSARY *Freedom is essential to Democracy. Food is necessary to life.*

EVIDENCE—TESTIMONY *The evidence established the fact that he was the assailant. Testimony,* the statement of witnesses, may or may not be evidence.

EX—FORMER *Ex* is the Latin prefix meaning out or out of. It is often used to mean former, as ex-president. *Former* is to be preferred where brevity is not essential, as it is in the newspaper headline.

EXPECT *see* Anticipate

EXTEND—OFFER—SHOW *He extended his arm. He offered* (or sent, not extended) *the invitation. He showed* (not extended) *the courtesies required by the occasion.*

FAIL *He failed to pick it up* means that he tried but did not succeed. *The automobile failed to hit the man* is not possible.

FARTHER—FURTHER *The museum is farther away than the library. We will discuss it further.*

FEWER *see* Less

FIX *He fixed the ornament to the wall* and *He fixed the boundaries* are correct. Such expressions as *I'll fix him, He fixed the motor* and *He is well fixed* are colloquial.

FORMER *see* Ex

FORWARD Not *forwards.* It is preferable not to use the final s on words like *homeward, backward, toward.*

FREQUENTLY *see* Generally

FURTHER   *see* Farther

GENERALLY—COMMONLY—FREQUENTLY—USUALLY   These words were defined by the grammarian George Crabb thus: *"What is commonly done is an action common to all; what is generally done is the action of the greatest part; what is frequently done is either the action of the many, or an action many times repeated by the same person; what is usually done is done regularly by one or by many. Commonly is opposed to rarely; generally and frequently to occasionally or seldom; usually to casually."*

GENUINE—AUTHENTIC   *The manuscript was traced to Shakespeare, thus proving it genuine. The book is authentic as far as it relates to the economic history of the country, but is inaccurate in dealing with the cultural development.*

GET   *see* Secure

GIANT—GIGANTIC   *Giant* is both noun and adjective; *gigantic* always an adjective. *The gigantic* (not giant) *missile is preferable.*

GOTTEN—GOT   It cannot be said that *gotten* is incorrect; it is merely falling to disuse in this country. *Got* is preferred, although the Anglo-Saxon verb is often so harsh that the softer Latin *obtained* is better. In such sentences as *I have got the book, got* is superfluous.

GUN—PISTOL   A *gun*, generally speaking, is a large weapon. *Pistol* is the general name of small firearms, of which the revolver and the automatic pistol are the common types.

HANGED—HUNG   Men are *hanged*; things are *hung*.

HAPPEN—OCCUR—TAKE PLACE   *The accident happened* (or occurred) *suddenly. The party took place as scheduled.* See also Transpire

HEALTHY—HEALTHFUL—WHOLESOME   *The animal was healthy. The climate was healthful. The food was wholesome.*

HISTORIC—HISTORICAL   *Historic* is something famous in history; *historical* is something relating to history. A book containing fictional characters from a past period is a *historical* novel; the Declaration of Independence is a *historic* document.

HUNG   *see* Hanged

IMPLICATE   *see* Involve

INAUGURATE—BEGIN   *The President was inaugurated. The project was begun* (not inaugurated).

INCUR   *see* Sustain

INDIVIDUAL   *see* Person

IN ORDER TO   Wasteful phrase. *He left home to go to the store* (not in order to go).

INVOLVE—IMPLICATE—ENTAIL   *He was involved in a long series of disputes. He was implicated in the crime. The project entailed* (not involved) *the levying of new taxes.*

JOIN TOGETHER   Redundant. *Join* means to bring two things together; the added word weakens the verb.

JUNCTURE—TIME   *At this juncture,* as meaning a critical time, is somewhat stilted. *At this point* or *at this time* are better.

KIND OF A   The article *a* after *kind of* is incorrect. *That kind of house.*

LADY—WOMAN   *Woman* is always used in newspaper writing unless *lady* is a title properly applied to an Englishwoman. *Female* for *woman* is a vulgarism.

LAST—LATTER   *Latter* is used in speaking of two things only; *last* is used in connection with more than two things.

LAWYER—ATTORNEY   A *lawyer* is a person admitted to the practice of law. An *attorney* is someone (not always a lawyer) appointed to act for another.

LEND   *see* Loan

LENGTHY—LONG   *Long* is preferred. *Lengthy* seems to be used repeatedly to denote a greater duration than *long* but it does not.

LESS—FEWER   *He bought less than a pound. There were fewer than twenty persons.*

LIMITED—SMALL   *A man of small* (not limited) *means. The slight* (not limited) *application of the law. The range of the gun was short* (not limited).

LIVE   *see* Reside

LOAN—LEND   *Loan* is the noun; *lend* is the proper verb. *He lent* (not loaned) *the book. A million dollars was loaned* is commonly used and is correct, but even in the financial sense *lend* is better.

LOCATE—SETTLE—SITUATE   *They settled* (not located) *on the river bank. The new city hall was located* (that is, its place determined) *on the hill. The city was situated* (not located) *between two rivers. The man was found* (not located) *at home.*

LONG   *See* Lengthy

MAJORITY   *see* Plurality

MAKE—EARN   *He makes shoes for a living. He earns* (not makes) *ten dollars an hour.*

MEAN—MEDIAN—AVERAGE   *Mean* is the sum divided by the number of components. *Median* is the midpoint in a grouping. They are both averages, but *mean* is the *average* most used.

MEDIA   The word is a plural. *The media are covering the election.*

NECESSARY   *see* Essential

NOVEL   *see* Unique

NOVICE   *see* Amateur

OCCUR   *see* Happen; Transpire

ODD   *see* Peculiar

OFFER   *see* Extend

OFF OF   *He fell off* (not off of) *the horse.*

ONLY   *see* Alone

OUGHT—SHOULD   *One ought to be honest. One should go to town today.*

PART   *see* Portion

PARTIALLY—PARTLY   *It is partly* (not partially) *done. It was done in a partial spirit.*

PARTY   *see* Person

PAY   *see* Settle

PECULIAR—ODD   *Speech was his peculiar gift. It was an odd circumstance.*

PEOPLE   *see* Person

PER—A   *Per* is often used in such phrases as *per day* and *per year*. It is better not to mix Latin and English. A *day*, *a year* should be used, or *per diem*, *per annum*.

PERSON—PEOPLE—PARTY—INDIVIDUAL   *Fifty people were injured. This people is peace-loving. This person* (not party) *is being sued. This party to the suit is a banker. This party* (group of persons) *is composed of bankers. Neither this group of persons nor this individual* (of the group) *should be sued. A strange person* (not individual) *arrived.*

PISTOL   *see* Gun

PLURALITY—MAJORITY   *He won the election by a plurality of 140 votes and a majority of 110 votes. He received 200, his nearest opponent 60 and the only other candidate 30.*

POISONOUS—POISONED—VENOMOUS   *The weed is poisonous. The snake is venomous. Poisoned* is a participial adjective and carries the active sense of the verb. One should discriminate between *poisoned food* and *poisonous food*.

PORTION—PART   *In the division of the estate, his portion was small. That part of the machine is rusty.*

PRACTICALLY—VIRTUALLY   *Practically* and *virtually* are used synonymously in newspaper writing to mean *almost*. In common usage this is not incorrect but a distinction would lead to a more agreeable variation. *This timber can be used practically as a foundation for the building* is a discriminating use of the word. *This seems to be virtually impossible but it can be done. The building is almost* (not practically) *completed.*

PREJUDICE—PREPOSSESS   *He was prejudiced against the plan. He was prepossessed in favor of the plan.* Bias could be substituted in either case.

PRINCIPAL—PRINCIPLE   *Principal* as a noun is the person who heads a school; as an adjective, the word designates what is first or foremost. *Principle* is always a noun and denotes a basic truth.

PROPORTIONS—DIMENSIONS   *The proportions of the building were pleasing. A rock of huge dimensions* (not proportions). *The close division on the amendment was held to presage opposition of some proportions* (strength) *when the resolution reaches the floor.*

PUPIL   *see* Scholar

RECEIVE   *see* Sustain

REFER   *see* Allude

REMAINDER   *see* Balance

RESIDE—LIVE   *Live* is always better than *reside*. So also is home or house for residence.

REVENGE   *see* Avenge

SAY   *see* Allege; Claim; State

SCHOLAR—PUPIL—STUDENT   *He is a scholar of world renown. This pupil has been under instruction for five years but is not yet ready for independent study. The students in the universities have shown seriousness of purpose. As a student of life he has learned much not taught in colleges.*

SECTION—DISTRICT   *Section* is used indiscriminately for region, district, neighborhood or vicinity. *This neighborhood* (or vicinity) *is composed entirely of shops. The legislation seeks the unity of the port district. This section of the country was a stronghold of the Prohibition forces. He surveyed the north-polar region.*

SECURE—GET   *The liner was secured to the dock. He got* (not secured) *the job.*

SERIOUSLY   *see* Critically

SETTLE—PAY   *They settled their dispute. He paid the bill.* See also Locate

SHOULD   *see* Ought

SHOW   *see* Extend

SITUATE   *see* Locate

SMALL   *see* Limited

SO   *see* Such

SO, AS   *see* As, As—So, As

SPECTATORS   *see* Audience

STANDPOINT—VIEWPOINT   *Viewpoint* or *point of view* usually is better.

STATE—SAY   *He stated the position of the government in a two-hour address. He said* (not stated) *that he would go.*

STOP—STAY   *He stayed* (not stopped) *at the hotel.*

STUDENT   *see* Scholar

SUCH—SO   *It was such a grave error that its effects can not be predicted* is now considered correct. Better *It was so grave an error that its effects can not be predicted.*

SUSTAIN—RECEIVE—INCUR   *Bread sustains life. He received* (not sustained) *injuries. He incurred* (not sustained) *losses.*

TAKE PLACE   *see* Happen

TESTIMONY   *see* Evidence

THINK   *see* Consider

TIME   *see* Juncture

TO   *see* And—To

TRANSPIRE—OCCUR   *It transpired long afterward that the incident had occurred at the secret meeting in Geneva.*

UNDER WAY   Two words. *By April the campaign was under way* (not underway).

UNIQUE—NOVEL   *The art of Benvenuto Cellini is unique. The hostess devised a novel way of entertaining her guests.* Most unique is never correct.

USUALLY   *see* Generally

VENOMOUS   *see* Poisonous

VERDICT   *A verdict* is a finding by a jury, not a judge. Judges render decisions, not verdicts.

VIEWPOINT   *see* Standpoint

VIRTUALLY   *see* Practically

WHENCE   *He returned whence* (not from whence) *he came.*

WHOLESOME   *see* Healthy

WOMAN   *see* Lady

PART TWO THE HEADLINE

6. WHAT THE HEADLINE IS

A HEADLINE WRITER who boasted that he was engaged in producing a literary art form promptly would be set down as an intellectual climber. Yet such a boast would not be without basis. For the headline is a form of expression having fully as many standards to be met and requirements to be filled as, say, the sonnet or the triolet, with the important additional one of visual form. The difference, of course, lies in the end-all—in one case it is beauty, in the other utility.

The headline's function is much like that of a commercial sample—the small tube of toothpaste distributed free at the dentists' convention, the guest-size bar of soap that you find in your hotel room. The headline is like the trial tube of toothpaste and, parenthetically, if it is set in sufficiently large type it is really free. The tiny tube aims at giving the prospective consumer accurate and complete information about the product, at giving the information in a quick and easy form and at presenting it so attractively that he will be impelled to form an attachment for the product. The headline's aim is the same: to present accurate and complete information quickly and attractively. The product to be sold is the news story.

Modern newspapers are designed to inform, and to inform as rapidly as possible. This purpose led to the development of the news lead—the opening of a story which packs into a paragraph or two all the essential information contained in the article. The headline carries the condensation process a step further. Where the lead speaks in terms of sentences and paragraphs, the headline speaks in terms of words. The headline is, in a sense, a super lead, and to facilitate rapid reading, display type is used. The large letters also serve to dress up the page typographically, but primarily they are employed to help the reader get at a glance what he wants to know.

As many readers keep posted on daily happenings almost entirely by scanning the headlines, the copy editor must incorporate as much information as possible in the head, must present it with unswerving accuracy and must emphasize the important point or points of the news. The technique of doing this will be taken up later. The present purpose is to discover what the headline is and how it developed.

Captions are probably as old as writing, but captions are not headlines. Titles for articles serve, for one thing, to mark off clearly where the articles begin. Often they apparently have no other purpose. Again in some cases they strive to give the reader an inkling of the information contained in the articles, but generally they accomplish this merely by labeling. In other cases titles are deliberately mysterious, alluring, seeking to tempt the reader into perusing what follows. Rarely are they both informative and alluring, as the modern headline frequently is.

In journalism of the English language we come across efforts to digest information and to present it in readily readable form as early as 1625. In that year a newspaper issued in London by a group of men, most prominent among whom was Nathaniel Butter, appeared with the following front page:

The
CONTINUATION
of our weekly
Newes, from the 24 of February
to the 2 of March

Wherein is contained the present state of Count Mansfield's
    Armse. The preparation of the Prince of Orange with
    the continuation of the siege of Breda.
The late surprisall of the Towne of Soeft by the Colonell
    Gent.
The warre-like preparations of Bethlem Gabor being aided by
    the Grand Signior
with the invasion of the Count of Thurne in Germany.
As also the proceedings which were lately made by the
    French forces in Veltoline.
Besides the great contributions which have beene given
to the King of Spaine to maintain the warres. With
divers other particulars.
From Rome, Venice, Naples, Millan, Savoy Germany,
    France, Denmark, the Low-Countries and divers other
    places of Christendome.

Aside from the obvious objection that these items do not head articles, they could in no sense be termed headlines. They do not divulge information, they tell *about* it. These are not the trial tubes of toothpaste mentioned before. They are merely the advertisements telling about the toothpaste. Wherein lies the distinction between the caption, or the label, and the modern headline? The chief point is the presence or absence of a verb. The distinction is between saying something and characterizing. The headline makes a statement, the caption calls names.

HOW HEADLINES DEVELOPED

Headlines are almost exclusively an American development. Newspapers in other parts of the world were until relatively recently content with captions. Therefore any sketch of the history of the headline concerns itself with American journalism.

The development of the headline in this country might roughly be compared to the development of the speech of an infant. The baby's first words, if psychologists and parents are to be believed, are simple nouns: "mamma," "papa," "spoon," "table." Quickly the young linguist begins to add adjectives to its vocabulary and says: "nice papa," "pretty spoon," "big table." In newspaper headlines the earliest stage is similar; the captions speak in terms of nouns and adjectives: "Foreign Affairs," "Tragic Accident," "Charge of False Pretenses." At this stage neither the baby nor the headline can be considered as really saying anything. We can discern in a general way what both are driving at. When the baby says, "pretty spoon," we gather that it is pleased; when the newspaper says "Tragic Accident," we gather it is shocked. But no direct statement is being made.

Finally, however, both become articulate, and the deciding factor is the addition of the verb. The baby now says, "'Gimme pretty spoon," "Nice papa come home," and the headline with its newly loosened tongue exclaims, "The Maine Blown Up" or "Two Held on Fraud Charge." Both have now come into their own, and the only difficulty is keeping the baby from talking too much and the headline from shouting too loudly.

Just when the headline began to assume its modern form cannot be told with any exactness, any more than it is possible to determine the moment when baby uttered its first verb. Just as the infant mumbles and squeals vague sounds that might be intepreted as verb forms before it actually speaks these forms clearly, so the headline made tentative, in some cases almost accidental, use of the verb before this came to be the recognized *sine qua non*.

From earliest times right up to the Spanish-American War days, the accepted headline form was the label. And this label was not infrequently a staple, the same one being used repeatedly. Aside from the usual departmental headings like

"Foreign Affairs" or "Diurnal Occurences," there were the "stock" heads used on the leading news stories. An examination of the files of *The New-York Times* for 1860, for example, shows that the heading "The Presidential Campaign" was used time and time again, and during the Civil War the latest tidings from the front were recorded first under the caption "The National Crisis" and later under either "The Great Rebellion" or "The Rebellion Record." It would not be fair to assume that the reader got no information from the heading, for these captions were always followed by subordinate divisions—often nearly a dozen of them—and it was in these parts of the headline that the verb occasionally cropped up, sometimes, it seems, almost against the will of the caption writer. On November 7, 1860, in the heading recounting the results of the presidential election, we find one bank that reads: "The North Rises in Indignation at the Menaces of the South"; and another declaring, "Abraham Lincoln Probably Elected President by a Majority of the Entire Popular Vote." The eight other parts of the head, however, are barren of verbs.

One of the earliest captions having the ring of a modern headline appeared in an "extra" of *The Boston Gazette* on October 26, 1781. The extra was nothing more than a single-page leaflet issued to bulletin a great event in the history of the colonies. In large type at the top were the words: "Cornwallis Taken!" The journalistic genius of the editor, Edes, in getting out an extra in the first place was confirmed by his choice of a caption, which, even according to modern standards, could not be improved upon. Even this, however, must be set down as a flash of genius and nothing more, for such captions were not the rule in those days. Again on June 11, 1865, *The New-York Times* carried a front page heading: "Steamer Sunk at Sea," which also smacks of the modern technique, but this, too, must be classed as a mere sport in the journalistic garden.

As indicated before, no line of demarcation is evident between the days of the caption and the days of the headline, but in a general way the war of 1898, during which the competition among newspapers to present the latest events speedily and luridly was intense, may be considered as the period that ushered in the headline that said something.

It was during this period, likewise, and in the years immediately preceding it that the headline was molded into its modern physical pattern. Before the Civil War, when the heading was nothing more than a caption, it was printed accordingly. Then in the intense days leading up to the war between the states, when the press underwent a rise in blood pressure and felt compelled to become a little more informative in its captions, large type and longer headings were used—sometimes they extended halfway down the page. But the type was a jumble of fonts, it still was comparatively small and it gave anything but a pleasing appearance, judged from today's point of view. The front page now contained three or four of these large heads, however, compared with the one or two it displayed in earlier days. By the time the Spanish-American War came along, the front page had assumed something of its present-day symmetry and the headlines had been dressed in more modern clothes, with tops of large display type and banks and crosslines that were in harmony.

Until this time, it must be remembered, the headline was kept closely imprisoned between the rules of a single column. *The Times*, it is true, had momentarily sawed through the bars on July 22, 1871, when it spread the headline (and story) of its Tweed Ring exposure across three columns, but this was exceptional. By the time of the blowing up of the battleship

Maine, however, the papers had become more liberal jailkeep-
ers and *The World* and *The Journal* in New York allowed the
headlines on this stunning event to roam the full width of the
page, thus introducing the familiar banner head of today. In
addition, tremendous type was used, larger even than we have
become accustomed to in present times. It remained for World
War I to give the multi-column head a standing in polite journalistic society.

Recently, some newspapers have returned to captions to
headline the news in acknowledging that their readers may
already be informed about an event by television. For example,
the day after the assassination attempt on Pope John Paul II,
on May 14, 1981, the *Boston Globe* carried the caption banner:
"Outlook Hopeful." The caption was followed by a headline
in smaller type: "Pope rests after surgeons remove 2 bullets."
But the headline format with a verb (or implied verb) continued to be used by most modern newspapers.

THE PRESENT TENSE

We have seen that the modern headline is distinguished by
the fact that it says something—it makes a complete statement
instead of merely characterizing. But in addition it speaks a
language of its own. This language is not "headlinese," a per-
verted speech, of which more will be said later, but is merely
pure English adapted to the requirements of headlining.

For one thing, the present tense is customarily used to describe past events. This usage is not something created by
headline writers, but is simply something borrowed from
everyday speech. The present tense is employed because it is
the tense of immediacy, because it is more vivid and hence
because it makes our trial tube of toothpaste more inviting
to the prospective buyer.

The corner grocery store has just been held up. In a frenzy the proprietor dashes to the street and shouts for a policeman. Presently Officer Murphy comes jogging to the scene.

"What's the trouble, Mr. Brown?" he asks.

"I've been held up," says Mr. Brown. "Two hundred bucks . . . my watch . . . he took everything. A fine police force. Well, why don't you do something? Don't stand . . ."

"Wait a minute, wait a minute. I gotta know what happened. Tell me about it."

"Listen, Murphy. This guy comes into my store. He asks for a pack of cigarettes. As soon as I turn to get it, he pulls a gun and sticks it into my back. He tells me to open the cash register. Then he cleans out the drawer, lifts my watch and beats it."

"O.K., Mr. Brown, I'll report it to headquarters."

This is a fair account of an everyday occurrence. Note how Mr. Brown describes the holdup. No past tense for him. He is living the scene over again. And incidentally he is making Officer Murphy live it with him. That, in a sense, is what the present tense in the headline does. It puts the reader on the scene, it makes him a participant in the action, it brings the events into immediacy.

That is the prime reason for using the present tense, but there is another. In most instances verbs in the present tense are shorter than those in the past, and space is always in demand in the headline. It takes fewer letters, for example, to say "Man Robs Grocery" than to say "Man Robbed Grocery."

OMISSION OF MINOR WORDS

So the use of the present tense to describe past action is one characteristic of our headline language. Another characteristic, which is more obvious to the ordinary reader, is the omission of nonessential words, chiefly articles. This practice has a tendency to give the headline telegraphic speed, and hence to make it more vivid. But contrary to a prevalent impression among headline writers themselves, the effect of speed is not the object of omitting words; it is rather a happy byproduct. Words are left out in headlines simply for the sake of economy, just as they are in telegrams. To pretend there is any other reason is as idle in one instance as in the other.

Still another characteristic of headline language is the use of short words, mainly of Anglo-Saxon derivation. And here again the space requirement is the commanding factor.

Obviously, then, limitations of space impose a distinct handicap on the headline writer. He is expected to put on an intricate juggling act in a five-foot square cubicle. The wonder is that he can do it at all, much less do it well. In the next chapter we shall see why the space is so restricted, and then we shall set about discovering how the copy editor performs his feat.

7. HOW THE HEADLINE LOOKS

HEADLINES are limited on the east and west by column width. In the vertical direction their form is definitely fixed by patterns—patterns that vary for different newspapers and for different kinds of heads used by any one newspaper, but that remain the same for any one type of head on any one newspaper. These two restrictions are what set the bounds of the cubicle within which the copy editor stages his juggling tricks.

TYPOGRAPHICAL PATTERNS

While headline patterns show diversity throughout the United States, they have at least one feature in common. The topmost part of the head is set, almost without exception, in display type, while the succeeding parts alternate between small and large type or between small, light type and large, heavy type. Put in another way, alternate parts of the head, beginning with the topmost section, are chosen for emphasis, typographically at least.

All the forms in which the parts of a headline are set may be reduced to five basic classifications: drop or stepped lines, inverted pyramids, crosslines, hanging indentation, and flush-left. In addition, some papers employ two or more lines set flush to both margins, but this might almost be considered a variation of the drop line.

In the drop or stepped line form, the lines are of the same length, but are symmetrically staggered like a flight of steps.

If there are two lines, the first is set flush to the left-hand margin and the second to the right-hand margin; if there are three lines, the first is flush to the left-hand margin, the second indented from both margins and the third flush to the right-hand margin. Sometimes the flight has four and even five steps.

The inverted pyramid may include any number of lines, within reason, from two up. In this form, the lines following the top line taper; each line is shorter than the preceding one.

Crosslines are simply single lines of type. They may be set either to extend across the full width of the column or "centered."

The hanging indentation form, like the inverted pyramid, may include any number of lines within reason. The first line is the longest and the succeeding lines are indented at the left, each by the same amount, but are flush with the first line at the right. In this form the succeeding lines are said to hang from the first. While it is not necessary that the final line extend all the way to the right-hand margin, the typographical appearance is better if it does.

In the flush-left form the lines of the topmost part of the head are aligned close to the left-hand margin and are allowed to run ragged at the right. This form was devised to make the writing of the headline easier, less confined by typographical restrictions. For the succeeding subordinate part of this kind of headline, various patterns have been tried. Some of them are not typographically successful; they have a tendency to drift uncomfortably in space. The banks seem to require either anchoring to one of the margins or stabilization by rules above and below them.

The following illustration will help in visualizing the first four of the five forms previously described.

DROP LINE FORM
LOOKS LIKE THIS

While These Lines Illustrate
the Appearance of an
Inverted Pyramid

AND THIS IS A CROSSLINE

Hanging Indentation Is Set
Like This and It Is Best If
Last Line Goes to Here

Incidentally, the illustration, if taken as representative of a headline, also shows the most common uses to which the typographical forms are put, that is, how they are employed in the various parts of a headline. It is not at all unusual, however, for drop lines to be used where the crossline now is, nor for the crossline to be employed as the topmost part. The illustrations on page 104 show four typical headlines, including all five typographical forms that have been described.

Two other typographical designs should be mentioned. One is simply a single line of type that may extend over many columns. This is called a ribbon and is used by newspapers that stress horizontal makeup. It is especially serviceable when a story has to be spread over a wide, shallow space on the page.

The other additional typographical design includes a subordinate line above a normal headline. This line, usually set flush to the left-hand margin and sometimes underlined, is called a kicker or a snapper or an eyebrow. It is sometimes used as a departmental designation such as "Theater News" or "Book Review." Other times it is used to include a subsidiary fact in the head, as in the example.

120 Planes to Fly From U. S.

Air Force Sets 'Exercise'
In the Far East Next Week

TERMINOLOGY OF THE PARTS

We have been referring to the "topmost part" of the headline and the "succeeding parts." Let us now give these various sections names so that we may refer to them more conveniently. In some newspaper offices every part of a headline is called a "deck." Other offices have a more precise system which we shall adopt. In these offices the word deck and its synonym "bank" are restricted to the subordinate parts of the headline having two or more lines. The topmost part of the head—the part that is set in large display type—is termed, logically enough, the "top." The parts of the head between the decks or banks, the parts set in more emphatic type than the decks, are usually styled "crosslines," even though they may not be crosslines in the typographical sense, but may be set as drop lines. This terminology, in addition to its advantage of being slightly more specific, conveys a better sense of what the parts referred to look like. Henceforth, then, we shall speak of the top, the first bank or deck, the crossline and the second or last bank or deck.

Two Men Shot As They Attack D.C. Policeman

**Officer Also Hurt
During Struggle
At Playground**

COURT WIDENS POLICE POWER IN SEARCHES

**Allows Rummaging in
Suspect's Home**

Rain Threatens Fast Field in '500'

Spotlight To Be Focused
On Jones's Turbocar
For Possible Trouble

APPEALS FOR HONESTY

**DR. WILLIAN F. KEUCHER
SPEAKS TO BAPTISTS**

**Central Seminary Graduates
Are Advised to Be
Themselves**

The top of the headline is, as has been noted, usually set in display type; it is the part that catches the eye first. It traditionally was set entirely in capital letters, although nowadays many papers use bold upper- and lower-case letters. Banks are customarily set in upper- and lower-case letters, while the crossline may be either in capitals or in capitals and small letters.

Virtually every newspaper office has a headline schedule, a chart showing samples of all the headlines used by that paper. The various heads are designated by letters or by number or, in some cases, by combinations of both. The largest single-column head, for example, might be styled an A head or a Number 1 head, the next largest a B head or a Number 2 head and so on. A number is often used to indicate the width of the head: A 3B head, for instance, would be a B head set three columns wide.

In electronic journalism, the practice of specifying the head for the composing room has been replaced by electronic commands in the computer system assigned to the particular head style and size. The makeup editor or news editor will specify what type of head is desired and the copy editor will then write that head on the computer, using the appropriate formats.

THE UNIT-COUNT SYSTEM

In any given size and style of type, the number of letters and of spaces between words that a line will accommodate is rigidly limited. For each headline the size and style of type are a given factor and it is the task of the copy editor, therefore, to make the lines fit the space. To accomplish this, he is equipped with a magic key—a key that will serve him on any newspaper for which he happens to be working. This key is simply a system of counting out the lines by units.

Printed letters are not all exactly the same width, although with certain exceptions they are approximately so. The following lines, each of which contains ten letters, show at a glance the relative widths of some of the letters:

```
AAAAAAAAAA
BBBBBBBBBB
CCCCCCCCCC
MMMMMMMMMM
WWWWWWWWWW
IIIIIIIIII
JJJJJJJJJJ
mmmmmmmmmm
wwwwwwwwww
iiiiiiiiii
llllllllll
ffffffffff
```

Obviously M and W are wider than other capital letters, just as m and w are wider than other lower-case letters. Likewise, I and J and i, l and f are narrower than normal. It is also obvious that capital letters in general are wider than small letters. These differences are recognized in the unit-count system.

Here is how the system works:

When a headline is set in upper and lower case, that is, in capital letters and small letters, the lower-case letters are generally counted as one unit each, except for m and w, which are counted as one and a half units each, and i, l, t and, in some styles of type, f, which are counted as half a unit each. The upper-case letters are counted as one and a half units each, with these exceptions: M and W are counted as two units each, I and J as one unit each. Figures, which are about the same size as capital letters, are counted as a unit and a half each, except for the figure 1, which is counted as a single unit. Most punctuation marks are considered to be a half unit each. Naturally, spaces between words must be included in the line count and they are arbitrarily set down as half units even though in the actual setting of the line they may be wider or narrower.

When a headline is set entirely in capital letters the system is even simpler. All letters except the M, W and I are counted as one unit each—M and W, of course, are counted as a unit and a half each and I as half a unit. All figures are counted as a unit each, except 1, which is counted as a half unit. Punctuation marks and spaces between words are counted as a half unit each.

That is all there is to the copy editor's magic key for making lines fit. Thus equipped he can enter any newspaper office, get a headline schedule, determine the maximum counts for

the lines of the various heads and be prepared to write headlines that are satisfactory, typographically.

Let us try counting a headline in upper- and lower-case
letters to put the system into practice. Here is the head:

**Fliers Join
Sham War**

And here is how it is counted:

	F	l	i	e	r	s	J	o	i	n	
Count	1½	½	½	1	1	1	½	1	1	½ 1	= 9½

	S	h	a	m	W	a	r	
Count	1½	1	1	1½	½	2	1 1	= 9½

Now let us try a headline made up entirely of capital letters:

**1,500 MEN FIGHT
ARMY SHAM WAR**

Here is how it is counted:

	1	,	5	0	0	M	E N	F	I	G H T	
Count	½	½	1	1	1	½	1½ 1 1	½	1	½ 1 1 1	= 13

	A	R	M	Y	S	H	A M	W	A	R	
Count	1	1	1½	1	½	1	1 1	1½	½	1½ 1 1	= 13½

"BROKEN" AND SHORT HEADLINES

The important thing a copy editor wants to know about a headline he has never tried to write before is the maximum count for each line. For he knows he dare not exceed this limit even by so much as a half unit. If he does exceed it, the headline will "break." And a "broken" headline, that is, one that is too long to fit within the allotted bounds, is a cardinal sin in headline writing, because it cannot be used in the paper and must be rewritten, usually by a makeup man and often hastily at the moment of going to press.

While the minimum count is not so rigid as the maximum, it, too, is important because of the extremely unpleasing typographical effect that results if the lines are too short. Note the poor appearance of the following head:

MEN TO HOLD
SHAM WAR

The importance of the appearance of the headline must not be minimized. Our sample tube of toothpaste is never soiled or partly folded up or encased in a torn box. Neither must the headline look skimpy or crowded or asymmetrical. If an inverted pyramid is called for, it should converge evenly from the top. If drop lines are being written, they should balance—the steps at both ends should be equal. Balance is achieved of course, by writing lines of equal length. The lines need not be of precisely the same length, but they should be within, say, a unit of equal length. If there is too great a discrepancy

between the lengths of the lines, again unpleasing effects result, as the following heads illustrate:

| MEN FIGHT | 1,500 MEN TO JOIN |
| SHAM WAR TODAY | SHAM WAR |

In the bank of a head the copy editor has a little more
leeway. Since the count is rarely given in terms of lines that
fill the column completely from rule to rule, the copy editor
can usually slightly exceed the count that is given without
danger of a "break." As a matter of fact, the count specified
for banks is usually only an approximation and most often is
set forth as a count by letters or even by words, rather than
by units. Nevertheless, of course, there are limits for banks.

The headline writer, then, is engaged in a sort of word game
in which he is trying not only to make big ideas fit into little
spaces, but also to dress them in pretty clothes. His wits are
constantly being challenged by the ever-present bogey of Maximum Count, and to win out he must be in command of
armies of short, pithy words and hosts of synonyms. When
one word fails him, he must be prepared to throw another or
a whole phrase into the breach. In addition, his battles must
be won quickly for he has many to wage before he reaches
deadline.

His problem, however, is obviously not merely one of getting
words to fit, but of getting suitably short words that say the
right thing. He is dealing with ideas as well as with words. And
since the function of words is always to communicate ideas,
what the headline says transcends every other element of it.
It is to this subject that we are now ready to turn.

8. WHAT THE HEADLINE SAYS

A HANDFUL of bouillon cubes represents a comparatively large pot of soup in compact form—all that is lacking is the water, which is its bulkiest part, but the essence is there. Similarly, a headline containing a few words gives a handy condensation of a news story that is a stick, half a column or eight columns long. In each case it is a question of boiling down to the essentials.

The top of the headline contains the main highlight of the story. Since it is the most conspicuous part and the part that is read first, the copy editor must present the essence of the news there before he goes further. And it makes no difference whether the top is an eight-column line of 120 point type followed by two or three banks, or whether it is a single line of boldface agate with no banks at all—the top tells the story. The banks and crosslines, if any, elaborate and add facts.

In presenting the kernel of the news, the top must tell the story at hand and tell no other. This is another way of saying it must be specific. Headline space is too precious to be wasted on vague words and generalities.

To illustrate what is meant by a headline's telling one story and no other, let us suppose that an article coming to the copy desk recounts that a banker, who had parked his automobile on a hill without setting the brake, was standing in front of it when the car rolled, knocking him down and slightly injuring him.

The beginner might be tempted to write as his headline: "Man Is Injured by Automobile." The head certainly could not be attacked on the ground of accuracy. There is nothing in it that is wrong. On the other hand, there is not enough in it that is right. It must be remembered that in any urban community men are injured by automobiles by the dozens, so that the foregoing headline might apply to any one of several stories. It does not tell one story and no other. It is too general.

A "nose for news" is every bit as necessary in a copy editor as it is in a reporter. What the copy editor must ask himself about every story that comes before him is: "What is the news in this story? What makes it different from other stories?" Only in that way can he make his headlines appear fresh and interesting. What, then, makes our automobile story different from the general run? Obviously it is the fact that a man was run over, not by someone else's automobile, as is usually the case, but by his own. How much better it would be to write as the head: "Banker Run Over By His Own Auto." Incidentally, we have made our headline more specific by particularizing "banker" instead of generalizing "man."

DISCOVERING THE NEWS

How does the copy editor go about writing headlines? It is imperative that he first edit the copy. This sort of close reading fixes the facts in his mind and gives him time to digest them. But there is another reason why the copy must be edited first. If the copy editor writes the headline at the outset, he may later find, on editing the story, that he is compelled for one reason or another to eliminate or alter facts that he has already included in the head. This necessitates patching up the head and means extra work and loss of time. It is decidedly unworkmanlike and unprofessional to attempt to write the headline before the copy has been edited.

Once the story is in final shape the copy editor sets out to determine its salient point—the point he is to include in the top of the head. He does this by mentally stripping the story of its unimportant details and piercing its comparatively copious verbiage to discover its fundamentals. What does this story really mean? In what would the reader be chiefly interested? What makes the story different? These are the questions that lead him to the point.

The kernel of the news is not always to be found in the lead, because sometimes reporters do not recognize it themselves. The copy editor must always exercise independent judgment on the story. He must be able to discover the news where the reporter, perhaps because he is too close to the story or because his perception is faulty, has overlooked it. In addition to good judgment, the copy editor should, of course, have a complete background of the current news so that he can tell promptly what is fresh and what has been told before, what is important and what is trivial.

If the news is buried too far down in the story, it is the copy editor's duty either to reorganize the copy so as to give it more prominence or to suggest that the story be rewritten. But in any case he must discover what the outstanding point is.

Usually this news point can be phrased in one short sentence. That is what the seasoned copy editor does, consciously or unconsciously, preparatory to writing the head. It is a good plan for the beginner to frame this sentence either mentally or on paper. The sentence will be too long, of course, to be fitted into a headline, but it will form a good working basis and will leave the mind unencumbered by nonessentials.

Let us see how this plan works out. Suppose we are required

to put a single-line head, with a maximum count of thirty
units, on the following story:

BORDEAUX, France, Nov. 23—Live perch rained from the sky
when a waterspout broke over Bordeaux Saturday. The downpour
lasted less than thirty seconds, but so many fish fell that motor cars
were halted. Housewives gathered up the fish in baskets and basins.

Interesting though the facts of this story are, we obviously
cannot include them all in a single-line head. We must, therefore, select the outstanding ones and eliminate those that are
subordinate. The important and unusual information in the
story is that "live perch rained from the sky during a waterspout
at Bordeaux." This, then, is our "news point sentence" that
will form the basis of the headline. The task now is simply one
of paring the thought down to thirty units.

Eliminating articles and turning the sentence into the present tense—headlines, it will be remembered, employ the present tense to refer to past action—we have: "Live perch rain
from sky during waterspout at Bordeaux." This is still much
too long, however, and we shall have to do some drastic cutting. Suppose we eliminate the waterspout idea. "Live perch
rain from sky at Bordeaux." This line, we find; counts 32½,
or 2½ units too much, but we are now within striking distance
of the headline. The problem now is not to cut out precisely
2½ units and make the count exactly 30, but to reduce it so
that it will be 30 or under. The word "live" seems to be the
most likely victim, so let us discard that. Then in polishing the
head we may decide that the word "perch" is not quickly understandable, and so we make it "fish."

FISH RAIN FROM SKY AT BORDEAUX

The count is 27, well within the maximum, yet not too short.
The headline covers the important and unusual angle of the

story. And it attracts and informs the reader. In short, it fills
every requirement.

In the foregoing story the headline point was readily apparent, and in the head it was necessary simply to set it down
and let it go at that; we had no room for elaboration. Let us
now turn to a story from an earlier time that is a little more
complex and for which we are called upon to write a headline
consisting of a top and a bank. We will assume that the top
is to consist of two drop lines of capital letters with a maximum
count of 18 units each, and the bank is to be an inverted
pyramid of three lines in which the first line has a count of
28 letters (not units this time) and the two other lines call for
counts proportionately shorter.

Here is the story:

What is described by builders and railroad men as a "remarkable
engineering feat, in many ways unique," will be carried out soon, it
was disclosed yesterday by the New York Central Railroad Company,
in the construction of a new viaduct as part of the $150,000,000 West
Side improvement project.

The railroad intends to bore through the Bell Telephone laboratory
building at Bethune and Washington Streets and lay its double tracks
through the building between the second and fifth floors without
disturbing the laboratory equipment and delicate instruments housed
in the eleven story structure.

To carry out this plan the New York Central has purchased from
the telephone company perpetual rights to air space along the Washington Street frontage of the building. The railroad has contracted
to build the foundations and enclose the viaduct in such manner that
trains will not disturb the workers or their instruments.

Sound deadening materials will be used in the walls enclosing the
viaduct and the tracks will be laid so that vibrations will not be transmitted.

Since the first paragraph is the most natural place to look for the news point, let us examine it. If we boiled it down to a news point sentence we should get something like this: "New York Central Railroad will perform a remarkable engineering feat." A headline built on this sentence, however, would smack of the caption of Civil War days: "Remarkable Engineering Feat." Even an exclamation point would not help it. It would be a case of calling names instead of making a statement. The head would not be informative. We shall have to look further then for our news point.

What we want to tell the reader in this headline is something of the nature of this "remarkable engineering feat." The second paragraph discloses this, and from it we can frame a news point sentence somewhat as follows: "New York Central Railroad will bore through the Bell Telephone laboratory building without disturbing the delicate instruments in it." Fitting all this information into our two drop lines is a large order, but is it necessary to get it all in? For a railroad to tunnel through a building is a striking feat in itself and we may safely concentrate on that one point for the top of the head.

The cat is now out of the bag. In trying to get at "what the story really means," we have hit upon an acceptable phraseology for the head in the sentence just above: "Railroad to tunnel through a building." Writing it out in two lines we find that the first, "railroad to tunnel," counts 16½ units, while the second, "through a building," counts 16. Since our maximum is 18 units for each, the lines will fit easily. We are now ready to write the bank.

It must be remembered that the function of the bank is not to repeat in different words what has been said before. Rather, its object is to elaborate and add facts. Taking the case at hand, we might be tempted to write the bank as follows:

NEW YORK CENTRAL PLANS TO BORE
THROUGH STRUCTURE TO
LAY ITS TRACKS

While it is true that the top is thus elaborated in one particular, identification of the railroad, the rest is merely a paraphrase of the top. The copy editor must constantly bear in mind that what is expected of him is not simply to write words—any words—that will fit and give a pleasing typographical appearance; the headline is expected to be informative.

Two obvious points of elaboration are needed in this bank—identification of the railroad and of the building. And at least one point of added information should find a place in the deck—the fact that the engineering project will not disturb delicate instruments in the building, a fact that we included in our news point sentence, but were forced to crowd out of the top. When all this has been squeezed into the bank the completed head might read as follows:

RAILROAD TO TUNNEL
THROUGH A BUILDING

New York Central to Pierce
Phone Laboratory Without
Jarring Equipment

When the head contains more than one bank, a greater degree of organization of the facts to be apportioned among the several parts is necessary, so that the important ones may receive a proper display and the less significant ones may be relegated to the less conspicuous parts of the headline. Let us try next a four-part head consisting of a top of two drop lines with a maximum count of 15 units each, a first bank in the form of an inverted pyramid with a count of 22 letters in the first line, a crossline of 21 units and a last bank, also in inverted pyramid form, with a count of 22 letters in the first line.

The following is the story for which we are to write the head:

A gaunt gray fox, brought many years ago from the Western plains to a cage in the Bronx Zoo, clawed and bit one of a group of small boys yesterday afternoon. The child had inserted his right hand trustingly between the bars to offer the animal a morsel of food. The boy, Herbert Bloomgold, 5 years old, of 765 Garden Street, was rushed to Fordham Hospital, his right forearm badly clawed and the little finger of his right hand fractured.

Unnoticed by park employees, the boys had scrambled over a barrier of rocks right up to the bars, which at the rear of the cage are not screened.

The fox was coaxed to the bars and the Bloomgold boy inserted his hand. The animal snapped its jaws, catching the lad's finger, and thrust a paw through the bars, digging its claws into the arm.

Two park employees, Andrew Mergner and Edward Fury, heard the boy's screams, ran to his assistance and freed him. At the hospital after the wounds had been dressed the boy received an injection to prevent rabies.

There should be little difficulty in framing the news point sentence for this story. It would read about like this: "A fox in the Bronx Zoo clawed and bit a 5-year-old boy who offered it food." Reducing the sentence to headline dimensions, the copy editor might write as the top: "Fox Bites Boy, 5, at the Bronx Zoo." This assuredly tells what happened, but it seems to leave something to be desired. For one thing, we get a slight suspicion that the second line—"at the Bronx Zoo"—is mere "padding," that the words were put there more to fill out the line than for any other reason. For another thing, the story has a "human interest" touch that is omitted from the head and would without doubt greatly improve it if included. This is the boy's trusting offer of food that resulted in the accident—

the "biting-the-feeding-hand" motif. Why not, therefore, make an effort to find room for this angle in the top? If we could in some way include the zoo idea in the first line, we should have the second line available for the human interest information. How about "Fox in Zoo Bites Boy, 5"? Too long. "Fox in Zoo Bites Boy." Still too long. "Zoo Fox Bites Boy." This line is 15 units and hence will just fit. Now we are ready for the second line: "Offering It Food." This counts 14 units and is probably satisfactory from the point of view of appearance, but there is ground for one slight objection. To the reader who takes in the head at a glance there might be some ambiguity as to which noun is referred to by the participle "offering." Perhaps this objection is hypercritical, but it would be better to phrase the head so as to preclude any possibility of misunderstanding; so that the meaning is apparent instantly. The line could be written, "Who Offers Food." This permits no uncertainty and incidentally we find that it counts 14½ units and therefore balances our first line nicely. Thus we have the top:

ZOO FOX BITES BOY
WHO OFFERS FOOD

ORGANIZING THE FACTS

With the top of the headline out of the way, the next step is to organize the remaining facts for the rest of the head, and the following principles may be laid down:

The first bank elaborates the top and adds the next most important facts after those included in the top.

The crossline sets forth a striking and important subordinate fact.

The last bank finishes off the head with whatever information of value remains.

To apply these principles practically, the copy editor surveys the facts left over after the top has been written and notes the best ones for use in the first bank, but at the same time reserving one good one for the crossline. He then proceeds to write the various parts of the head in the order in which they occur. He never should write the crossline before he has completed the first bank, nor should he proceed to the last bank until the crossline is safely out of the way. This *modus operandi* is necessary in order to avoid awkward repetitions of words and sentence structures, and to insure the proper grammatical organization of the head—points that will be taken up in the next chapter.

Marshaling the facts of our fox story, we note that the animal snapped at the boy and clawed him through the bars and that the boy's finger was fractured. Since the fracture of the finger gives the reader a clue to how much damage was done and demonstrates vividly the power of this wild beast, it would make a striking point for the crossline. Let us therefore reserve this fact and use others for the first bank.

Was there anything in our news point sentence that was crowded out of the top? Two items: identification of the zoo as the one in the Bronx, and the boy's age. These facts, then, should find place in the first bank as items that elaborate the top. The beginner might think of setting them down bluntly somewhat as follows: "It happened in Bronx Park and the boy's age is 5." But the experienced copy editor is not so wasteful of words; he inserts such facts more economically, including them incidentally while he conveys his additional information to the reader. He would probably write:

> **Animal in Bronx Park Snaps**
> **at Hand Thrust Into Cage**
> **and Claws Child, 5**
>
> ————

That seems to cover the points apportioned to the first bank and we may now go on to the crossline. Since the space restrictions of the crossline are rigid like those of the top, it would be well to frame another news point sentence as a basis for it. The count, remember, is to be 21 units. The sentence might be made to read: "The fox fractured one of the boy's fingers with its jaws." The word "fox" is superfluous, since we have it in the top and since the word "animal" is the subject of the first bank. We could therefore begin the crossline with a verb and there would be no doubt as to the subject. Well, then: "Fractures Child's Finger." But the count is 21½ units, ½ too much, and an excess of half a unit is no less impossible for the printer to fit into the line than is one of ten units. Moreover, as we have the word "child" in the first bank, let us avoid repeating it. The line may be remedied as follows: "Fractures Lad's Finger." Now the count is 20 units, which will slip nicely into the space.

The last bank, in addition to rounding up the remaining information, may also elaborate the crossline if this is necessary. Perhaps in this case it would be well to tell what other injury the boy received. What else is left? Two park employees heard the boy's screams, ran to the spot and set him free. The bank, then, might be written as follows:

> **Arm Lacerated—Cries Bring**
> **Two Attendants on Run**
> **and They Free Him**
>
> ————

Here is how the completed headline would look:

ZOO FOX BITES BOY WHO OFFERS FOOD

Animal in Bronx Park Snaps
at Hand Thrust Into Cage
and Claws Child, 5

FRACTURES LAD'S FINGER

Arm Lacerated—Cries Bring
Two Attendants on Run
and They Free Him

Note that there is no waste of space in this head. Every part of it is used to give information and the story is covered so completely that the hasty reader can get all the essential facts by merely scanning the headline. That is the principal function of the head: to tell the story.

Most headlines cannot be this complete simply because they do not contain so many parts. Many newspapers use only a single bank in their main heads and many others use none at all. This situation makes it the more imperative that the copy editor pack the most information possible into the lines that are available.

Mention was made in the previous chapter of the kicker that is included in some headlines. When it is not used as a mere departmental heading its function is like that of the bank of a head: it elaborates and adds information to the main head. But it should be borne in mind that despite the fact that it appears at the top of the headline it is a subsidiary element. It is set in smaller type than the main head and does not catch the reader's attention immediately. Therefore it should never contain the principal news of the story. Moreover, it should not be used for a qualification that is essential to the main head. For example, it would not do to write as the main head, "Jones Guilty of Murder," and write as the small kicker, "District Attorney Alleges." This not only would be misleading but also would border on dishonesty.

BULKY, COMPLEX STORIES

If all news articles were as simple and direct as those already used as illustrations, the copy editor's task would be far simpler than it is. But he is constantly confronted with more abstract and, at the same time, more complicated stories which he is expected to compress into a few words. Not infrequently, for example, is he called upon to take some message that it required a statesman or a clergyman days to prepare, thousands of words to convey and hours to deliver, and reproduce the gist of it in half a dozen words within ten minutes. Many stories by their sheer bulk almost overwhelm the copy editor, so that he hardly knows where to begin his job of compression. Stories that contain too much information and too many good news points are one of his tribulations.

An elephant is big, and so is a swarm of locusts. Yet the methods employed to kill them are entirely different. The elephant is most readily dispatched by sending a steel-jacketed bullet into a vital part—the brain, for example. But the same method would hardly be efficient in the case of the locusts—imagine the farmer sitting on a fence, rifle in hand, sniping away at individual insects! One of the most efficacious means of killing off the pests is to blanket them with insecticide.

These two methods illustrate how the copy editor goes about bringing down the big ones. Bulky stories may be roughly classified as of either the elephant or the locust type. In the case of elephant stories, where there are several good news points of approximately coordinate interest and importance for which no common denominator can be found, the copy editor trains his gun on a vital spot and bags the story with a single shot. In the case of locust stories, where several good news points can be lumped together because they contain some common factor, the copy editor writes a headline that blankets the story.

Conventions of various kinds furnish the majority of these two types of stories. Forums in which many different subjects are taken up would usually be of the elephant classification, while symposiums on a single subject would often be of the locust kind. But these groupings are by no means invariable. A symposium on a single subject frequently could be treated as an elephant story, with better results in the headline.

The Elephant Type. To make clear the distinction between the two types of stories, let us examine an example of each. The following is the beginning of one of the stories:

WASHINGTON, Oct. 5—Protective measures to minimize hazards in traffic, ranging from blind flying to automobile accidents, were discussed today during the third day's sessions of the Annual Safety Congress of the National Safety Council.

To illustrate up-to-date police methods of dealing with accidents, a real collision between automobiles was staged, including the taking of photographs by the traffic officer as well as statements from witnesses.

A better spirit of cooperation in the direction of true highway safety among motorists, drivers and owners of commercial motor vehicles and state regulating agencies was urged by Joseph G. Jones, Commissioner of Motor Vehicles of New Jersey.

Harold P. Smith, president of Metropolitan Airlines, told the meeting of the Safety Council's aeronautical section that the safety record of aviation in this country was an achievement worthy of the highest commendation.

Here several points are presented, too many to be handled easily in a headline. Nor can the copy editor find any generalization to put into the headline that will not be too dull to do the story justice. He therefore treats the story as of the elephant type and shoots at a vital spot. He writes the head as follows:

CAR CRASH STAGED FOR SAFETY FORUM

The Locust Type. The other story used for purposes of illustration concerns a conference of major industries held at Columbia University, at which twelve speakers from various countries proposed international business agreements for the stimulation of trade and, incidentally, for the furtherance of world peace. A spokesman for Germany advocated a shipping compact; a French automobile manufacturer suggested an international automobile cartel; the president of Columbia University emphasized the international character of the world's economic problems; a representative of Great Britain appealed for cooperation among nations, and so forth.

Almost any one of the addresses would make a meaty story in itself, but they are all fused into a single article. To build the headline on one speech would not give the reader a proper idea of the scope of the conference, nor would it afford the other addresses the treatment they deserve. Here, then, is the locust type of story and the best kind of head to write for it is one that blankets it. This is a possible head:

> **12 LEADERS URGE NATIONS TO SPUR TRADE AND PEACE**

This headline is general enough to encompass the whole story, yet not too vague. It illustrates what can be done if the copy editor can find a common denominator.

Pigmy Elephants. All elephants are not big, nor are all stories that fall into the elephant classification freighted with important facts. On the contrary, some elephant stories are distinctly of the pigmy variety; they contain a succession of comparatively insignificant facts all seeming to be on a dead level. In such cases, although a vital spot may be difficult to find, the copy editor uses a rifle rather than a spray gun, and hence the stories must be classed as the elephant type.

The vital spot may be an unusual quotation or a striking thought. A "headline phrase" or a "headline word" is what the copy editor seeks. He resists to the utmost the temptation to compose a routine headline that these stories customarily offer.

Some years ago an Italian Foreign Minister visited the United States, and while he was here the newspapers tried to report the daily doings of his wife. But she refused interviews and at all times avoided the limelight. The result was trivial copy, little more than a timetable of her goings and comings. In one story it was recorded that the Signora went on a shopping tour to buy gifts for her friends and children. After having visited several stores she went to the toy department of a shop that was bright with Christmas decorations. She gazed around delightedly and exclaimed: "These toys are charming." Then she bought a little breakfast set for each of her two children, a mechanical army tank for her little boy and two dolls for her little girl. The rest of her day was routine.

Vital points are hard to find in a story like this. But the alert copy editor notes that this woman who had granted no interviews did at last say something that could be quoted. He therefore seizes his rifle, takes aim, pulls the trigger, and presto:

OUR TOYS 'CHARMING'
TO VISITING SIGNORA

And a pigmy elephant has bitten the dust!

Annual reports of institutions and speeches on normally uninteresting subjects—in short, stories that are printed more as a matter of record than as a matter of interest—form the most likely stamping grounds for pigmy elephants, and the copy editor should constantly be on the watch for them to avoid writing dull headlines.

Elephant stories far outnumber locust stories and in all cases where a clear-cut news point is lacking the copy editor will do well to assume that the article is of the elephant type until he has proved it to his own satisfaction to be otherwise. For the attempt to blanket a story in the head is too often likely to produce generalities and vagueness.

It has been noted before that headline space is too precious to be wasted on generalities. The injunction for copy editors is "Be specific!" From one point of view this requires telling one story and no other, as already indicated. From another, it demands the technique of the elephant story—picking out a salient point rather than indulging in a sweeping statement. But in addition it involves packing the headline with precise facts and figures.

If it is a budget story that is under consideration, the phrase "Big Budget" is not nearly so good as "$5.2 Million Budget"; if it is a robbery story "Valuable Jewelry" is inferior to "$83,000 in Jewelry"; if it is a wreck story "Train Accident" is far less satisfactory than "Train Is Derailed." In each of these examples the inferior form makes a characterization that the reader could deduce for himself from the specific information that the better form sets forth. If "$5.2 Million Budget" is stated, the reader knows it is a "big" budget and receives additional information as to the amount; if he reads "Train Is Derailed" he gets all the information that "Train Accident" would give him and more besides.

Compare the following two headlines from the point of view of the information they convey:

MANY ARE KILLED   15 WOMEN KILLED
IN A BUS SMASH-UP   AS BUS RAMS POLE

These two headlines have about the same unit count, yet the one on the right contains three more items of information than the one on the left. It tells that "women" were killed, it specifies "15" of them and it reveals how the accident happened: "Bus Rams Pole."

THINGS TO AVOID

Editorializing. The border line between making characterizations—such as "Big Budget"—and editorializing is not always clearly defined. For instance, suppose the headline referred to a "High Budget." The copy editor would leave himself open to a charge of expressing an opinion instead of stating a fact. The question would involve what interpretation would be placed on the word "high" and, although the copy editor might protest that he meant merely "big," others might get the impression he meant excessive. There is no provision for explanatory footnotes, and so the headline must say clearly what it means.

Whereas characterization suffers simply from inadequacy, editorializing is undesirable because it does not adhere to the facts and may easily lend itself to coloring of the news. Opinions are as much out of place in the headline as they are in the news story—there is only one place for them and that is on the editorial page. The headline must reproduce only what is contained in the story; it must say just what the story says.

John Jones, we will suppose, tells the local rotary club in a speech that "the United States is going to the dogs." Our reporter writes his story with this as the lead. Perhaps the copy editor finds it difficult to fit both Jones and the United States into the headline and so he throws up his hands and writes:

UNITED STATES
IS GOING TO DOGS

This is an example of a headline that does not say what the story said. The story recounted that John Jones had said "the United States is going to the dogs." The headline says flatly on its own account that the United States is in this unfortunate condition. It is not a news headline; it is an editorial in display type. The beginner always has a ready solution for this problem.

"I'll put quotation marks around it," he says.

That, however, is not a solution; it is a makeshift; it is an attempt to patch up bad work. Assuming that the reader pays any attention to the quotation marks—and there is no assurance that he will notice them—he still will be in doubt as to their purpose. The quotation marks will not themselves indicate that a speaker or writer is making the statement; for all the reader knows they may indicate merely that the quoted words constitute an editorial slogan of *The Daily Bugle*.

The headline must definitely indicate that someone is responsible for the statement. Either we must get Jones's name into the headline or, if this is not practicable or if the name is not sufficiently well known to justify its use, we must include some verb that will leave no doubt that someone other than *The Bugle* is making the declaration. Here are two possibilities:

JONES SAYS NATION   NATION IS VIEWED
  IS GOING TO DOGS   AS GOING TO DOGS

Libel. Saying in the headline exactly what is said in the story is also a foolproof way of avoiding libel, if we assume that the story has been so edited as to free it from committing this offense. Libelous headlines usually arise from the overlooking or ignoring of qualifying facts in the story.

Just as a fair and true account of proceedings in a court of record is privileged from the point of view of libel, so a headline that summarizes this account fairly and accurately is not libelous. If a witness in a proceeding calls Brown a forger, the reporter does not write bluntly: "Brown is a forger," nor even "Brown was revealed as a forger." He writes, "The witness testified that Brown was a forger," or "The witness accused Brown of forgery." Similarly, the headline in reproducing these facts does not say, "Brown Is Forger," or "Brown Revealed as a Forger." It says "Witness Accuses Brown of Forgery," or "Witness Terms Brown a Forger."

There is a difference between saying "Robber Is Held" and "Man Held as Robber." In the first case the headline brands the prisoner as a robber before he has been tried. In the second case it merely reports the charge that has been lodged against him without attempting to indicate whether he is guilty or innocent.

In general it must be remembered that space restrictions of headlines are no defense against libel. If anything, greater care should be taken to guard against libel in writing heads than in writing stories, although this is by no means intended to countenance any laxity on the part of a reporter. The headline gives statements greater prominence than does the story and, since it is inevitably read by more persons, the libel is aggravated, actually if not legally.

So, in addition to being informative and specific, the headline must take no liberties with the facts in the story; it must say just what the story says.

Thus far we have described the size and nature of the cubicle in which the copy editor performs his difficult juggling feats and we have discussed the material he is called upon to juggle. If that were all, it would still be a good trick. But there is more. We are now ready to take up further restrictions he is expected to meet and the methods he employs in keeping his gleaming words and ideas spinning in air.

9. HOW THE HEADLINE SAYS IT

STRICTLY SPEAKING there are only two rules for writing a headline: it must fit and it must tell the story. A head that does not fit is of no use at all, and one that does not tell the story is useful only in a decorative way.

But while there are only two rules, many customs, usages and guides that have persisted because sound reasons underlie them have acquired almost the force of rules. Although it must be borne in mind that they are not inflexible, that in extreme cases they are subordinated to the two rules, the best headlines comply with them.

THE ALL-IMPORTANT VERB

It has been noted that a headline is distinguished from a caption by the fact that it makes a statement instead of merely labeling. It has been further pointed out that the key to this distinction is the presence of a verb in the headline. We may therefore take it as one of our first guides that every part of a headline should contain a verb.

The headline verb may be either explicit or implied. The previously cited head, "Our Toys 'Charming' to Visiting Signora," for example, contains the implied verb "are." The word order frequently decides between mere label and a statement containing an implied verb. Compare, for instance, "Victorious Troops" to "Troops Victorious."

Not only should the head contain a verb, but in the top it is considered preferable to put the verb in the very first line. Since the first line is the one that gives the reader his initial impression of the story when the head is seen at a glance, it should, if possible, be more than just a label line. When it contains a subject and a predicate, while it may not make a complete statement, it at least provides an excellent start for one. "Fox in Zoo Bites" conveys more information and gives a better start to a statement than "Fox in Bronx Zoo." In the latter instance the reader must go on to the next line to get a clue to the nature of the story.

Perhaps it seems a small point to distinguish thus between successive lines in the top, but it must be remembered that one aim of the head is to inform quickly and any device, such as the one just discussed, that serves this end is valuable. Carrying this idea still further, the head strives to set forth in the first line at least one of the elements that "make the story," something that identifies the subject matter instantly. When feasible, the "blind" top line should be avoided. The following heads illustrate the point:

| DEATH CLAIMS | TWO DIE IN CRASH |
| TWO IN AUTO CRASH | AS AUTO HITS BUS |

The head on the left fills the requirement for a verb in the first line, but the line is blind. The reader must go to the second line to find the element that makes the story. In the head on the right, however, all the news is in the first line— it can be seen instantly.

Whatever the story, the copy editor should try to make the first line of the head a telling one, to insert a verb that sets it in motion and to include an identifying element.

Besides informing quickly, the headline, as noted previously, tries to deliver its message in attractive style. It seeks to be forceful, colorful, active. While in ordinary writing such qualities may be achieved partly by well-selected adjectives, in headlines there is usually little space to spare for these parts of speech. Here again the verb is all-important. A well-chosen, potent verb can suffuse the head with energy; a flat, colorless one leaves it limp and lifeless. The verb determines whether the headline contains "punch" or is dull.

Facts must under no circumstances be strained or exaggerated for the sake of using a forceful verb, but when the news itself is dynamic it is a mistake to employ any but a forceful verb. If a liner comes into port after a stormy voyage, with railings torn loose by waves and portholes smashed by pounding seas, it is inadequate to say in the head, "Liner Reports Storm at Sea." A more attractive and at the same time more informative head might be: "Liner Battered by Heavy Seas." The verb in this case pictures the story and gives animation to the head; the lines would be more likely to tempt the reader than would the other head, which merely records the fact that a ship encountered a storm.

Too much emphasis cannot be laid upon the necessity for choosing strong verbs and avoiding weak ones, for the verb more than any other factor is the key to a successful headline. In general it is well to shun parts of the verbs "to be" and "to have" as the principal verbs in heads; these two are the most obvious of the weaklings. Note in the following illustrations how headlines are brightened by replacing these weak verbs with stronger ones:

| JONES IS NEW MAYOR | CHILE HAS A GALE |
| JONES WINS MAYORALITY | GALE LASHES CHILE |

If we are trying to achieve vigor in heads through verbs, it follows that the active voice is to be preferred to the passive voice. And the copy editor takes cognizance of this, using active verbs whenever practicable. This suggestion, however, is qualified by the previous one that calls for including the important news element in the first line. If using the active voice necessitates dropping this element to the second line, it is better to reverse the order of the head and sacrifice telling the story actively to telling it quickly. Taking as an example an injury to Governor Jones of New York during a tour of the West, we might compose either of the following heads:

AUTO CRASH INJURES   GOV. JONES INJURED
GOV. JONES IN WEST   IN CRASH IN THE WEST

The one on the left employs the active voice but the one on the right puts the important news into the first line, telling the reader quickly what he wants to know. "Gov. Jones Injured" is, therefore, the preferable line.

FIGURATIVE WORDS AND CONSTRUCTIONS

Words are frequently used in a figurative or semifigurative sense to lend color to a headline, and this is good practice provided the figurative uses are not too hackneyed or do not exaggerate the facts. When a speaker opposes a project it is proper to say he "attacks" it if his opposition is really that strong. If a man merely casts a negative vote on a project it would be an exaggeration to say he "attacks" it. More will be said later about the use of "headline words." What is to be noted at this point is that figurative words, properly used, are among the legitimate ornaments the copy editor employs to make the headline more attractive.

Likewise figures of speech have their place as valuable adornments, but they too must be used with discretion. Improperly used, they may prove either ambiguous or ridiculous. Here is an example of a metaphorical structure lending strength and interest to a headline that might otherwise be prosaic:

**NAVY GROUP FIRES
A NEW BROADSIDE
AT U.S. ARMS PLAN**

On the other hand, let us consider the case of the governing board in some city which, after years of controversy, has finally voted to award a bus line franchise. The copy editor, striving to evolve a colorful head, might turn out this one:

**CITY BOARD RULING
GIVES CLEAR ROAD
TO JONES BUS LINE**

What is the matter with this headline? The trouble is that the figure of speech is too good; it is so apt that if the reader, by some not impossible chance, should take it literally the meaning would instantly become absurd. In the case of the head about the Navy men the meaning is purely figurative— the words do not conjure up a picture of the men touching off guns. But the bus headline might well suggest a gang of laborers clearing snow or debris or what-not off an actual road for the benefit of the lucky Jones Company.

Some stories are negative and others are tentative. This cannot be helped. But if the headlines written for them are negative or tentative they will lack force. And this usually can be helped.

Readers are not as a general thing interested in learning what did not happen or what is merely continuing to happen. Nor are they much interested in what may happen. What they want to know is what did happen and what will happen. Their desires in this respect give the copy editor his clue to writing positive heads, without in any way altering the meaning of the stories, on negative or tentative copy.

If a judge refuses to enjoin strikers, we do not say in the head, "City Does Not Get Injunction"; we say "Court Refuses to Enjoin Strikers," or "City Fails to Get Injunction." If a gathering of some kind is called off, for one reason or another, we do not say "Meeting Is Not Held Because . . ." but "Meeting Is Canceled Because. . . ." If Mr. Jones declines to become a candidate, we try not to say "Jones Not to Run," and substitute "Jones Refuses to Run."

Then there is the General-Grant-Still-Dead type of headline which should be avoided. Accomplishing this usually involves nothing more than discovering the elephant's vital spot. The head should not read "Murder Trial Continues," but should feature something that took place at the trial.

Avoiding the "may" head—the tentative one that says something may happen—is a little more difficult. But every effort should be made to do so, for the word "may" is among the most effective enemies of the strong headline. Unquestionably there are occasions when it is impossible to escape this construction, but in many cases words like "possible," "probable" and "likely" point the way out. In other cases it may be said that something "impends" or "looms" or that someone "warns of," "expects" or "fears" a contingency. And in still other cases the word "ready" will prove helpful. Use of the word "may" should be only a final resort when it is impractical to phrase the head any other way without twisting the meaning of the story.

In general the head that says something positive is more effective and more interesting than one that is negative or hesitant.

THE "SPLIT" HEAD

Each line in the top of a headline is treated more or less as a unit. It is generally understood that a word is never divided between two lines. What is not so generally understood is that according to the best standards integral grammatical structures likewise are not divided. If they are, the result is what is known as a "split" head. The split head is not to be confused with the broken head, which, as set forth previously, is one that is too long to fit the required space.

The eye in reading successive lines is compelled to pause ever so briefly and shift focus at the end of each line. If the content of what is read has a corresponding resting place, no matter how slight, at the end of the line, quick and comfortable reading is facilitated. It is on this principle that the avoidance of split heads is based.

The copy editor strives to achieve a clean break at the end of each line. If each does not express a complete thought, it at least stands on its own grammatical feet. The preposition is not placed on one line and its object on the next; the natural union of the two is preserved. When an adjective and noun are adjacent, they, too, are not parted, one on one line and one on the next. Likewise, the parts of a compound verb are not divided.

A few illustrations will make clear the distinction between a head that is split and one that is not:

| THIEVES ROB MAN IN | THIEVES ROB GUEST |
| A HOTEL IN MIDTOWN | IN MIDTOWN HOTEL |

The head on the left is split. The "in" as the preposition governing "hotel" should be on the same line with it. Some how we get a feeling of greater comfort in reading the head on the right. The word "in" dangling from the end of the first line in the other head produces an impression of slovenliness; the line does not appear to be polished.

Here is another illustration:

| JONES TERMED ABLE | JONES TERMED ABLE |
| GOVERNOR IN REPORT | IN REPORT ON STATE |

Exactly the same first line, yet one produces a split head while the other produces a satisfactory head. In the example on the left "able" is an adjective modifying "governor" and hence should not be thus parted from it. In the one on the right, however, it modifies "Jones" and the thought is complete in the first line. Again the split head creates a slight feeling of discomfort because the reader, subconsciously at least, expects the first line to stand by itself, only to proceed to the next line and find that he has still to include another word in the thought he took to be complete.

Words are not always what they appear to be at first. The copy editor must exercise care in determining exactly what part of speech each word in the head is and to make his adjustments accordingly. Sometimes, for instance, words that customarily are nouns occupy the role of adjectives in headlines. This duality may mislead the copy editor and cause him to split the head. The following heads provide an example:

| POLICE SOLVE MURDER | POLICE SOLVE MURDER |
| MYSTERY IN THE BRONX | OF PLUMBER IN BRONX |

In the head on the left "murder" is used in an adjectival sense and modifies "mystery." Hence the head is split.

Dividing parts of verbs is a common form of split head. Compare the following examples:

| NEW MISSILE WILL | NEW MISSILE GETS |
| RECEIVE TEST TODAY | FIRST TEST TODAY |

In some instances an adverb and verb are so clearly bound together that they amount almost to parts of a compound verb and therefore should not be divided. "Hold up," "shake up," "come in," "go on" and similar phrases are examples of such combinations. But here again the copy editor must discriminate between the adverbial and prepositional uses of the words. If the words "up," "in" and "on" used in the foregoing illustrations are employed as prepositions, they are kept with their objects rather than with the verbs.

The injunction against split heads applies only to the top, and to the crossline when it is more than a single line. It applies, that is, only to those parts of the head that are set in prominent type and hence are designed to be read at a glance. Splits in banks are not at all frowned upon. Nor are divided words objectionable in banks except in so far as they mar the typographical appearance of the headline; they should for this reason be kept to a minimum. Moreover, when the top contains three lines, many papers do not object to a split at the end of the middle line.

It is difficult to frame any thoroughgoing test that will let the copy editor know in all cases whether the head is split. It might. be said that if the first line of the top ends with a noun or a verb the head is not split. This is true, but it is not comprehensive, for the line could conceivably end with other parts of speech and not result in a split head. If we go back, however, to the principle of a resting place at the end of each line, which, we noted, formed the basis for the effort to avoid split heads, perhaps we can formulate a rough rule of thumb, as follows: If each line ends at a point in the headline where there might conceivably be a pause—even a slight one—were the head to be read aloud slowly and deliberately, the headline is not split.

Taking one of our first sample heads as an illustration, we might scan it as follows: "Thieves Rob—Guest—in a Midtown Hotel." Therefore, if in writing out this head we were to stop the first line after either "rob" or "guest," there would be no split. We could not, however, scan the head in this way: "Thieves Rob—Guest in—a Midtown—Hotel." Hence, if a line ended with either "in" or "midtown," the head would be split.

Many newspapers in which the lines of heads are so short as to make the phrasing of them a matter of extreme difficulty are inclined to be tolerant—perhaps too tolerant—of split heads. Other papers enforce a virtual prohibition of them. In both cases the clean-cut head that avoids a split is the ideal.

Somewhat akin to the split is the practice of stopping a line in the middle to take up a new thought. While this is generally considered a fault, the break is often necessary to tell the story more fully and, when this is the reason, it is acceptable. The following is an example:

SCHOOL BUS CRASHES
INTO TREE; THREE HURT

Although rules may well be subordinated to the effort to tell the story, it should be noted that the preferred practice in writing heads is to treat each line of the top as a unit and to make it self-sufficient, if feasible.

OMISSION OF THE SUBJECT IN THE TOP

Another by-product of the headline's principal function— to tell the story—is the occasional omission of the grammatical subject in the top. In some heads the first word is a verb. Since this construction is necessarily incomplete and since it is a sharp departure from ordinary speech or writing, it falls some- what short of being ideal. Nevertheless, when its use is re- quired to tell the news, it is distinctly preferable to a construc- tion that includes a subject but excludes the important point or points of the story.

Use of the subjectless head depends on the content of the story and the space exigencies of the top lines. It is permissible to employ it when both the subject and the predicate of the statement patently cannot be fitted into the head, and when the subject is not so important as the predicate or when it is obvious. Here is an example of how the construction is used, the top of the sample head being one that has a maximum count of 22 units:

STEALS PISTOL TO END LIFE

Jobless Stenographer Arrested for
Taking Policeman's Revolver

In telling this story it would be possible to write a top that would include a subject, but not without sacrificing the news, which the top of the foregoing head includes. In this case what was done—the act of stealing a pistol with suicidal intent—is more·interesting than who did it.

An example of a story in which the subject of the verb would be obvious, and hence could be omitted if space requirements demanded, would be the report of an indictment. Since only a grand jury returns an indictment, the subject could be left out of the top.

One restriction accompanies the subjectless head—a restriction that comes closer to being a hard and fast rule than any other of our guides for writing headlines. The restriction may be stated as follows: When the top of the head, lacking a subject, begins with a verb, the subject of that verb must be the first word or phrase in the bank immediately following, and the subject and verb must be in agreement grammatically.

The following illustration shows how this requirement is carried out:

KNOCKS OUT BIG THIEF	KNOCKS OUT BIG THIEF
New-Born Baby Inspired Him, Says Ambitious Policeman	Policeman Seeking Promotion, Says Baby Inspired Him

In the head on the left the ambiguity, arising at first glance, as to the subject of "knocks out," results in an absurdity if the reader takes the subject to be "new-born baby." The head on the right leaves no room for even momentary misunderstanding. It is to be noticed that the subject of the verb "knocks out," i.e., "policeman," begins the bank and is in proper agreement with the verb.

GRAMMATICAL CONSTRUCTION

If a subject is given in the top, succeeding parts of the head may begin with verbs "hanging" from that one subject, but here again they must agree with it grammatically.

When any part of a head other than the top begins with a verb, the reader may usually rightfully assume that the subject is the last preceding one mentioned. If the copy editor fails

MAYOR SALUTES
FLAGPOLE SITTER

Down With a Record of Six
Weeks, Medal Is Pinned
on Jones at City Hall

PRAISES 'FINE COURAGE'

Police Hold Back Autograph
Seekers Besieging Hero—
Clamor for a Speech

to take cognizance of this, the head is likely to be confused and halting. An example of the jumble that results when the subjects are not properly indicated, not to say when the English is faulty, appears at the top of this page.

What has been said about subjects and verbs indicates clearly that in many cases the parts of a head are regarded as interdependent. But there is a limit to this interdependence. The parts may properly be treated as separate sentences having the same subject. Except in rare cases, however, they should not be treated as parts of the same sentence. Since the several thoughts expressed are thereby rendered incomplete, the practice of having one part of a head "read out" of another is usually frowned upon. It should be pointed out, however, that a few papers have made this form of headline office style. An example of the headline in which one part reads out of another is this:

MAYOR PINS GOLD MEDAL

On Flagpole Sitter Who Came Down
with Record of Six Weeks

Sentences in ordinary writing occasionally begin with conjunctions like "but" or "and"; hence what has just been said is not to be construed as precluding the starting of subsidiary parts of a headline with such words.

AVOIDING REPETITION

Carrying a single subject down through the banks and cross-lines is acceptable, as indicated previously, but it should be noted that this may lead to monotony through repetition of the same construction. Just as in writing of other kinds we shun beginning four or five successive sentences with exactly the same subject and employing precisely the same grammatical structure, so in headlines we should guard against this kind of monotony, which detracts from their attractiveness. It can easily be avoided by casting one part of the head in the passive or active voice, as the case may be, or by interpolating the "he said" phrase in the midst of the indirect quotation, or by some other device that circumstances indicate.

Likewise to be avoided is the monotony arising from the repetition of words and names. It is generally considered bad practice to repeat in a head any word except the minor ones like articles and prepositions. But this prohibition can be, and often is, carried to a ridiculous extreme. There is no excuse for repeating a word that has an abundance of synonyms, but if the only substitute a copy editor can think of for "water" is "*aqua pura*," he would do better to repeat "water."

PUNCTUATION

Punctuation in headlines follows, in general, the ordinary rules, but in addition there are a few headline conventions. Periods are omitted in heads except when used in abbreviations. When two thoughts are included in the top—the equivalent of two sentences in ordinary writing—they are separated by a semicolon, thus:

GALE LASHES CHILE;
DAMAGE IS SEVERE

When two thoughts appear in a bank they are separated by either a semicolon or a dash, depending on the style of the particular paper.

The comma is employed in the regular way and, in addition, is used in exceptional cases to take the place of the word "and." The following is an example of this use:

PRESIDENT, MAYOR
RALLY PARTY AIDES

An interrogation point placed at the end of a head to indicate doubt or speculation on the subject matter is viewed with disfavor. Its use in this way, which seems to be rapidly disappearing, is illustrated in this head:

JONES TO RUN FOR MAYOR?

Aside from the fact that it indicates laziness or lack of ingenuity on the part of the copy editor, the construction has the same objections as the tentative head—the "may" head—discussed previously.

In the top of a head the dash is used rarely, as, indeed, it is in other forms of writing. The principal objection to it is that it mars the typographical appearance of the head. A few papers permit its use in this way:

DEMOCRATS WILL WIN
IN THE FALL—JONES

Besides being typographically unpleasing and abrupt to read, this usage, too, suggests that the copy editor has surrendered to a makeshift as the easiest way out of a troublesome situation. It should be avoided.

Quotation marks have a variety of uses in headlines and, excepting the comma and the semicolon, are the most frequently employed form of punctuation. Most papers use single quotes in the tops of heads because they occupy less space, and either single or double quotes in banks, depending on style. Quotation marks are used, of course, to enclose exact phrases or words employed by a speaker, or by a statement or report. Further, they are used to set off slang. Still further, they are used to soften a word that might be harsher than is intended, or to indicate that the truth of the word used is an open question on which the newspaper rightly does not take sides. An example of this last-named use is as follows:

JONES CITES 'PROOF'
OF CITY CORRUPTION

In some instances quotation marks are used to actually reverse the meaning of a word, or at least to give it a double meaning, as in the following head:

'DEAD' MAN APPEARS
AT HIS OWN FUNERAL

In any paper except a sensational one, exclamation points are used scarcely ever. When they are used it is to follow an actual exclamation quoted from some source or to punctuate a bulletin or an event of astounding historic importance. Such events, needless to say, are rare.

NUMERALS

Numerals, of course, are commonly used in headlines and usually the more precise they are the better.

Parenthetically it may be said that in instances where two figures are given in a story to indicate an estimated range, it is usually better to use the more moderate one in the head. If a crowd is estimated between 7,000 and 8,000 persons it is preferable to use 7,000; if the value of the jewelry stolen is placed between $70,000 and $80,000, the $70,000 figure is the better for the headline. When a prisoner receives a sentence from three to five years, his sentence, for headline purposes, is three years, since it is unlikely that he will serve any more than that. If a flight is made in eight hours and fifty minutes and the exact time cannot be included in the head, it is better to say "less than nine hours" than "about eight hours."

In general, moderation of this kind is likely to win the reader's confidence in the newspaper's reliability, while a tendency to make figures sound big and important on every possible occasion leaves him with an inclination to discount, not only the figures, but everything else he reads.

STORY ELEMENTS TO STRESS

Time. Since headlines employ the present tense in speaking of past action, the introduction of past-time elements like "yesterday" or "today" makes for awkwardness and produces the impression that something is awry, which, grammatically speaking, it really is. The "when" of the story is, barring exceptional cases, an unimportant piece of information for headline purposes. Besides, it can be taken for granted; the reader assumes that his morning paper is presenting the news of yesterday or last night and that his evening paper is telling him what happened today or last night. The time element not only is superfluous, but in addition occupies space that might better be used to tell the news more fully.

Note the clumsiness of the head, "Thief Kills Man Yesterday." It is incongruous and should be avoided.

Future time involves no such difficulty and its use in head-lines is justified. While a newspaper's past is restricted, usually to the preceding twenty-four hours, its future is indefinite. Therefore it frequently is best to specify future time. Hence the time fits naturally with the tense used, which may be either future or present. If there be any doubt as to the propriety of employing the present tense, it need only be recalled that this is well-established in ordinary usage. When we are asked, "When does John return from Europe?" we reply, "He arrives next Monday." Likewise, in a headline it is proper to say, "Jones Opens Campaign Today," or "Jones Opens Campaign Next Week," and the reader will not misunderstand, nor will he feel any incongruity.

Location. Just as the reader takes certain things for granted about the "when" of the story, so he makes assumptions about the "where." Unless the location of the story is set forth some-where in the head, either specifically or by implication, he assumes it to be the town where the newspaper is published. It is not always possible, nor desirable, to "locate" the story in the top; but this should be done in some part of the head, when the story is not a local one, to avoid giving the impression that it is local. Even in local stories, specifying the part of town is necessary, especially when the locale is an important ele-ment in the news. In New York, for example, a holdup in fashionable Park Avenue is a better story than one in East 112th Street, other things being equal.

The "Who" of the Story. As to the "who" of the story, it is bad practice to identify the principals by race, nationality or religion in the head, unless this information constitutes a rel-evant part of the news. While it is entirely proper to write, "Irish Honor St. Patrick," or "100 Blacks Protest Alabama Lynching," it is not proper, barring exceptional circumstances, to write, "Two Italians Rob Bank President," or "Negro Stabs Wife and Two Children."

Inclusion of names, too, requires the exercise of discrimination. There is one type of story, however, in which the headline writer's course is always clear—the obituary. It hardly need be pointed out that in the obituary the name is the news; hence it must in all cases appear in the top of the headline.

In other news stories, however, as a general rule names should not be included in a head unless they will be readily identified by readers in the town in which the newspaper is published. This, of course, eliminates use of names in headlines on minor police stories in towns of considerable size. When stories continue over a period of time, it frequently happens that names, at first unknown to readers, come to be recognizable and to have a certain news value, so that their use in headlines is proper. It is not possible to say at what stage of a running story it is correct to begin using a man's name in a head instead of identifying him in some other way. This depends upon how frequently and how prominently the name has appeared; it is a matter upon which the copy editor must use his judgment.

"FIRST-DAY" AND "SECOND-DAY" HEADS

Mention of running stories brings us directly to a consideration of the distinction between "first-day" and "second-day" heads. After a story has "broken," headlines on its successive developments may identify it by a name or a phrase. An investigation of city corruption may become a "graft inquiry" or the "Jones inquiry." Soon the name Jones by itself is sufficient identification.

The second-day head should not repeat the first day's facts. Let us consider a typical story. We shall assume that a dancer of no great prominence has been killed, and the head on the story is as follows:

SHOT KILLS DANCER
IN HER STUDIO HOME

On the next day the suspicions of the police turn to an actor who was friendly with her and a general alarm is sent out for him. Compare the following heads on this development:

POLICE HUNT ACTOR   POLICE HUNT ACTOR
  AS DANCER IS SLAIN   IN MURDER OF DANCER

The head on the left, it will be seen, does not give the impression of a second-day story, but rather suggests two almost simultaneous events: the slaying and the hunt. In its second line it repeats the first-day occurrence. The head on the right, however, stresses the second-day angle and at the same time includes the necessary information about what happened on the first day. By its assumption of knowledge of the previous story, it emphasizes the fact of a new development.

On the other hand, let us suppose that the slaying and the hunt actually were both developments on the first day, that is, that the dancer was killed and the police immediately started searching for the actor. In that case the head on the left would be a proper first-day head, while the one on the right would be inferior because of its "second-dayishness."

Banks, too, should conform to first-day or second-day requirements. Assuming we are to write a bank for the foregoing second-day head, "Police Hunt Actor in Murder of Dancer," we might evolve either of these two:

Learn He Was Friendly With   Learn He Was Friendly With
  Her—Girl Killed By Shot   Girl Who Was Killed by
    in Studio Home   Shot in Studio Home

Obviously the one on the left suffers from the same fault as the previously discussed top: it repeats, as fresh, facts that were told to the reader the day before, when it says, "Girl Killed by Shot in Studio Home." The other bank includes this same information, but refreshes the reader's memory of it without giving him the impression that it is trying to present something old as something new. The use of subordinate clauses, illustrated by it, is a handy aid to the copy editor, enabling him to slip old but necessary information into the head without the reader's being unduly aware of it, since the information is coupled with fresh facts.

"HEADLINESE"

In a previous chapter it was noted that headlines speak a language of their own, and at the same time it was pointed out that this language is not "headlinese." That strange speech that corrupts good English cannot be too severely denounced, for headlines have a greater effect on everyday language than is usually suspected.

Headlinese arises from three main causes. One is the space restriction that compels excessive compression. A second is the vague desire on the part of some copy editors to make what they have to say "sound like a headline"; if it sounds too much like ordinary speech it must be discarded in favor of something less simple, less tame and, usually, less clear. In this particular the trend should be just the other way: to make the headline approximate straightforward English as much as possible. Only in this way will it tend toward greater clarity. A third cause of headlinese is the insistence of some papers that headlines be "jazzed up," that they have "punch." As has been pointed out, it is desirable that the head have color and force, but accuracy and clarity must never be sacrificed. If a headline does not communicate a thought, it is nothing more than a decoration. Headlinese manifests itself in a wide range of forms. It may appear in a conservative, but obscure head like this:

CLUB FIGHT BLOCKS
RIVER RAIL TUBE PLAN

Or it may explode in a racier head like this:

LOVE NEST RAIDED
IN WIFE SWAP PACT

In either case it amounts to little more than a succession of staccato words that are certain to perplex most readers, momentarily, at least.

Two characteristics of headlines are apparent in the foregoing illustrations. One is the disconcerting use of nouns in an adjectival sense. The other is the use of arbitrary symbols, such as "love nest," that appear nowhere outside the lurid headline.

Use of Nouns as Adjectives. It would facilitate matters if it were possible to say flatly: never use a noun as an adjective. Unfortunately, such a rule is not feasible. As a matter of fact, nouns may be and often are used properly in the sense of adjectives. The trouble in headlines lies in the fact that nouns are so frequently used in this way in series, as in the first of the foregoing heads; or in the fact that the nominative case is used when the possessive is intended, as, "club fight" for "club's fight," or in the fact that the noun is used as an adjective when it actually has a proper adjective form which, through carelessness or lack of space, is ignored, as "freak" for "freakish." What can be said, however, is that a noun should not be made to serve as an adjective when it has its own adjective form that conveys the proper meaning, or when its possessive case would be more proper. In general, the use of nouns as adjectives should be kept to a strict minimum and in any case should not take the form of a distressing concatenation like "river rail tube plan."

Headline Symbols. As to headline symbols, copy editors are too ready to coin them because they are labor-saving devices. Tabloids are the chief offenders in this regard, but they always have the excuse that symbols are the things most easily understood by their readers. Once again it must not be said flatly: do not use symbols. They have a legitimate place, provided they are readily understandable and reasonably dignified. Deprive your harassed headline writer of "shake-up" or "racket," and his lot would be harder than ever, while at the same time there is no assurance that his headlines would be more felicitous.

The current tendency, however, toward corruption of words for the sake of symbols is to be frowned upon. It may be inevitable, if undesirable, that a long word like "helicopter" will become "copter" in headlines, yet we may well draw the line if an attempt is made to chop off suffix as well as prefix and term the machine a "copt."

Ambiguous Use of Words. Another characteristic of headlinese is the ambiguous use of words. This characteristic is closely related to the misuse of nouns for adjectives which, in itself, often leads to ambiguity. Here is an example of an ambiguous head that smacks of headlinese:

JONES WILL FIGHT
HINGES ON BABY

Even the most alert of newspaper readers would probably be puzzled by this head at first until they discovered that "will" was being used not as a verb, but as an adjective and that the head referred to litigation over a testament. The fact that "hinges" is susceptible of two meanings only makes matters worse.

To avoid situations like this, the copy editor must take care to read his headline over from every possible point of view, weighing each word to make sure that it conveys only the meaning intended.

Overworked Words. Figurative words, as indicated before, are often helpful in injecting color into a headline. The only difficulty is that, with hundreds of newspapers being issued day after day, the figurative expressions soon become tarnished from too much handling. One by one, as they lose their original brightness, they are dropped, sometimes temporarily, sometimes permanently. Other words are found to be too bright to begin with, that is, they always exaggerate.

The word "flay," a favorite among some headline writers who use it when they are trying to "jazz up" the idea of simple criticism, means to skin. It is no wonder that the word is in disfavor for headlines. It is not necessary to go into the precise meanings of other pet headline words, but overworked words like hit, probe, cop, slap, nab, aver, rap, mum should be avoided. There are of course others, but this brief list is sufficient to indicate the type of word that is meant. As might be expected, the words that have suffered most at the hands of headline writers are the shortest ones. While several of the examples just given may have been forceful, expressive words at one time, for headline purposes they have become flat. Moreover, in their headline meanings, most of them are hardly ever employed anywhere but in a headline, and for this reason, together with what has been indicated before, they must be classed as headlinese.

So long as space remains a controlling factor in headlines, a comparatively few short words will be compelled to bear an inordinate burden. The situation is inescapable, but it can be somewhat alleviated if the copy editor exerts a little extra effort in the quest for a fresh means of expression. If he continually falls back on such routine words as "see" and "plan," his headlines are bound to be routine. A little extra thought will often point a new approach to his problem.

Abbreviations. Pick up a weekly newspaper in a very small town. Often its headlines will be found to be strewn with abbreviations, initials of all kinds which generally are unintelligible to the nonresident. Abbreviations, of course, make headline writing easy, but they also make headlines obscure. For this reason they should be severely avoided. A very few are necessary. It would be unreasonable to expect a copy editor to fit "Federal Bureau of Investigation" or "Young Men's Christian Association" into the ordinary headline. But when possibly a dozen or so exceptions are made, it may be laid down as a rule that abbreviations are taboo. This, of course, does not apply to abbreviations that are used commonly in ordinary writing—such abbreviations as those of titles like "Dr." and "Capt." when used before names, or of the names of states used after the names of towns as in "Trenton, N.J."

Slang. Slang is a common characteristic of headlinese. Some papers, especially tabloids, not only do not object to it but encourage its use, as a breezy language that comes closest to the understanding of their readers. In the more conservative papers slang has its place when the nature of the story demands it, but in other cases it should be shunned in favor of the proper English that the intelligent public rightfully expects the press to employ.

Excessive Omission of Words. To know what words may be

omitted in headlines is important in guarding against headlinese. Obviously words may not be dropped indiscriminately
when they will not fit into the specified space. If they are, the
result is cryptic language that either is impossible to understand or at least is something alien to good English.

Mention has been made of the use of the comma to indicate
the omission of the word "and," which in certain rare instances
is considered legitimate. The copy editor has not the license,
however, to extend the use of the comma to indicate the
omission of other words. Such a conglomeration as the following, for example, is indefensible:

SNOW TRAPS AUTOS,
GALE, FREEZING COLD

This head does not make sense; too much has been left out
of it.

What words, then, may be safely omitted from headlines?
To begin with, articles usually may be dropped. It should be
noted, however, that a prevalent impression that they *must*
be dropped to give life or speed to the headline is erroneous.
The headline aims to approximate ordinary speech, and thus
there should be no hesitancy in using "the" or "a" when it is
needed for clarity. Not infrequently the article is necessary to
avoid ambiguity or to make a statement more specific. Here
is an example:

JONES FINDS WORK
WAY TO SUCCESS

This head might mean either one of the two ideas expressed
specifically in the following examples:

JONES FINDS WORK   JONES FINDS WORK
A WAY TO SUCCESS   THE WAY TO SUCCESS

Obviously either of these two heads, depending on what the story says, is preferable to the first, because neither leaves any doubt as to the exact meaning.

Likewise it is patent that the following two heads mean two entirely different things:

MAN KILLS BOY AT PLAY   MAN KILLS BOY AT A PLAY

Adjectives usually are not necessary in headlines. When they constitute an important news element, however, they should be included. Titles, such as Doctor, Captain, Professor, used before names may generally be dispensed with. In addition, parts of the verb "to be," when used as auxiliaries in the passive voice, may be omitted. The headline may say either "Banker Is Hurt" or "Banker Hurt."

The "To Be" Rule. While parts of "to be" may always be omitted in the instance just mentioned, there are other cases in which they definitely must not be omitted. Let us consider as illustrations two headlines that phrase an identical thought in two different ways:

ROBINSON ASSERTS   COUNTRY SOUND,
COUNTRY SOUND   ROBINSON ASSERTS

An experienced copy editor recognizes instantly that the head on the left is wrong while that on the right is correct, but if asked to explain why, he will probably reply that—well— it's just a question of the sound of the thing. This answer is correct so far as it goes; the head on the left does sound wrong. But that is not an adequate explanation.

The verb "assert" and many others like it normally are followed by the objective case: we assert *a fact*, we say *something*. The ear trained to English therefore expects the noun following these verbs to be in the objective case. But in the headline under consideration, the noun "country" is not in the objective case, but in the nominative case: it is the subject of the clause "that the country is sound," which clause itself is the object of "asserts." We must therefore indicate that the noun is not in the case normally to be expected. How shall we do it? If we use the conjunction "that," we run counter to an unfortunate circumstance because the conjunction may be mistaken for a definite article. There is only one way: by using the verb of the clause—"is." The head therefore should read:

ROBINSON ASSERTS
COUNTRY IS SOUND

How about the other head cited, "Country Sound, Robinson Asserts"; why is that correct? The answer is simple. In English the first noun mentioned in a sentence is, virtually without exception, in the nominative case. Reading this head, then, we would normally expect "country" to be in the nominative case, which it is, and therefore no further indication is necessary.

Omission of this vital verb "to be" may sometimes lead to ambiguity. Here is an instance:

PHYSICIAN SAYS
PRESIDENT WELL

If "president" were taken to be in the objective case—the logical assumption—then the head would mean that the physician was a capable elocutionist.

The real objection to omission of the verb, however, is not based on the possibility of such an ambiguity, but rather on the awkwardness of the situation as explained before. To avoid this awkwardness, a rule may be laid down as follows: A part of the verb "to be" may not be omitted in a headline when it constitutes the principal verb in a clause.

The sole exception to this rule has already been noted in the discussion of the second headline illustration—the rule does not apply when the clause begins the sentence.

Difficulty over "to be" arises in clauses following such verbs as: say, deny, assert, allege, warn, contend, maintain, affirm.

It might be supposed that the verb "declare," since it is synonymous with "say," would fall into the same classification. Such is not the case, however, because "declare" has another meaning that is commonly employed in headlines. The following head is quite correct:

JONES DECLARES
COUNTRY SOUND

Here "declares" is used not as synonymous with "says" but in the sense of "pronounces" or "terms." "Country" is therefore in the objective case in accordance with our normal expectation.

Knowing when to include the verb "to be" and when it may be omitted will help the copy editor to avoid many an awkward and amateurish head. It is a point that is not generally understood, even among veterans at the copy desk, and a little study to master the principles just set forth will repay the effort.

SPECIAL HEADLINES

Feature Heads. Headlining feature stories is a ticklish task. It is here that the copy editor feels the pinch of his space restrictions the most. To attempt to convey humor, pathos or color in the painfully few words allotted, and at the same time to communicate the necessary information that imparts the news, tax his ingenuity to the utmost.

Unfortunately, there is no known way of giving any great amount of intelligent guidance in how to write a feature head.

It is just about as feasible to do this as to instill a sense of humor into a humorless person or to teach a student fine writing. The most that can be done is to lay down a few very general principles and leave the rest to taste and talent.

Feature stories may roughly be divided into four classes: color stories, romanticized stories, pathetic stories and humorous stories. Each, of course, calls for a different kind of headline, but a common principle applies to all. The headline should be in key with the story; it should be a sample clipped from the same bolt of cloth that went to make up the story; in short, it should be appropriate. This does not mean that in headlining a funny story all that is necessary is to write a funny head; it means that the head should reflect the same type of humor that is to be found in the story. The head should epitomize the spirit of the story.

Under no circumstances should the copy editor tolerate headlinese in the feature head. Here if anywhere it must be firmly put aside, because one key to a successful feature head is a fresh manner of expression, which headlinese precludes. In fact, the copy editor would do well to avoid thinking in headline terms at all in composing the head, so far as this is possible.

The Color Story. The color story, by which is meant the account that is mainly descriptive, calls for the same technique in the head that applies to the writing of the story itself. When we experience an event we are simply absorbing sensations, we are in contact with it through some or all of our five senses. Descriptive writing attempts to reproduce the experience for one who did not have first-hand knowledge of the event, and its method is to try to establish a similar contact with the senses. The color headline employs the same method; it uses sense words. While its appeal is usually restricted to the senses of sight and hearing, it can, in its limited way, paint an impressionistic picture.

The Romanticized Story. Romanticized stories are those in which the news contains a strong flavor of the unusual, the thrilling or the exciting. A jewel robbery is just an ordinary news story, but if the clues point definitely to a deft Jimmy Valentine the story might lend itself to more romantic treatment. When a liner crosses the ocean, the story is of no great moment, but if a man crosses alone in a yawl there is material for what might be (and, alas, usually is) called a saga of the sea. In either case the headline obviously should not be a routine news head, but should dramatize the facts in the same spirit in which the story does. Writing such a head involves going back to first principles; that is, picking out the unusual news point; but in addition it involves, as was indicated before, expressing the news in a fresh way.

Suspense. Suspense and the headline method are, of course, directly antithetical. It is possible on rare occasions to achieve suspense in a headline by saving the point of the story for the very last part of the head, but since at best the suspense must be extremely brief this plan is not often successful. The head that omits the point altogether and compels the reader to delve into the story to discover it is sometimes legitimate, although it must be confessed at once that such a headline is typographical decoration and little more. In most instances this type of head is not necessary and the reporter's complaint that the head "gives away" the story is not valid. A distinction must be made between suspense and mere surprise. The interest in Greek drama was not spoiled for the audiences by the fact that they knew perfectly well how the plays would end. Likewise in many news stories nothing is lost through knowledge of the outcome; the interest lies in living the incident through with the characters. Often, in fact, the interest is heightened by the agonizing or happy knowledge of the inevitable outcome.

An illustration is furnished by the following delayed lead story:

CRESTWOOD, N.Y., Oct. 8—For almost a year Eugene C. Tobin, 18 years old, of 85 Oakland Avenue, here, had maintained an unblemished record for promptness in arriving at the offices of the New York Central Railroad at 370 Lexington Avenue, New York, where he was a clerk.

This morning he did not respond as quickly as usual to the knock on his door by Mrs. J. W. Wallen, with whom he boards. He left the house with only a few minutes in which to catch the 7:41 train. He ran down the hill to the station. The train was pulling out.

Tobin reached for the guard rail to pull himself into the train. He missed it. His clothes caught in a contact shoe of the car and he was dragged under the wheels. He died ten minutes later.

Without in any way spoiling the effect of the story, the headline could tell the news as follows:

**PUNCTUAL MAN KILLED
AS HE RUNS FOR TRAIN**

*Clerk Who Had an Unmarred
Record for Promptness
Falls Under Wheels*

In slenderer stories, however, where the surprise twist is the only meat the story contains, it would be folly to reveal this point in the head. But such stories are uncommon.

The Humorous Story. Headlining the humorous story demands careful exercise of taste and discrimination. The copy editor may as well resign himself at the outset to the fact that try as he may, in nine cases out of ten his humorous headline will be about as funny as a professor's classroom joke or an anecdote told before the Academy of Arts and Letters. Brevity may be the soul of wit, but it is poison to headline humor.

When a funny story is set before a beginner in copy editing, usually the first idea that pops into his head is to write a rhymed headline. Now, there is a place for a rhymed head; probably one out of every five thousand stories calls for such treatment. It has its place only when it reflects the tenor of the story. Let us illustrate. The following is the lead of one such story in five thousand:

Ellis Parker Butler, humorist, who lives in Flushing, Queens, has lately taken an interest in the street naming and house numbering system now being carried on throughout the borough. He discussed the subject with Charles U. Powell, engineer in charge of the topographical bureau, and yesterday suggested a rhyme, which, like the old rhyme for remembering the number of days in the month— "Thirty days hath September"—he hopes will become useful.
Mr. Butler's jingle was as follows:

> In Queens to find locations best—
> Avenues, roads and drives run west;
> But ways to north or south, 'tis plain,
> Are street or place or even lane;
> While even numbers you will meet
> Upon the west and south of street.

And this was the head:

> **VERSE GIVES A MEANS**
> **TO GET ABOUT QUEENS**
>
> *E. P. Butler Rhyming System*
> *Guides All Folks if Street*
> *Plans Twist 'Em*

That head is appropriate. The story is made to order for the rhymed head. A jingle, however, is out of place for a story that carries no suggestion of rhyme. Oddly enough it is more difficult to write an appropriate head that is funny than it is to compose a rhymed head. The rhymed head is comparatively easy for anyone with even a slight flair for verse.

With the rhymed head ruled out, the novice at desk work usually turns next to alliteration to get his humorous effect— not the subtle alliteration that properly ornaments poetic writing, but the Peter Piper school of alliteration-with-a-vengeance. The result is almost always sophomoric. The advice here is to forget alliteration altogether.

A pitfall in composing the humorous head is the temptation to write one that is "blind," that gives the reader no clue whatsoever even to the nature of the story, much less to the information it contains. It must be remembered that a headline, no matter how sidesplitting, is worthless if the reader is compelled to go back to it after having read the story to discover what it means. Unless it means something to begin with, its purpose is defeated.

"Lily-painting" is something else to be avoided. In many stories the facts are funny enough to stand on their own feet. A mere recital of them conveys all the humor that is necessary or possible. All the bright euphemisms, allegorical allusions and figures of speech in the world would not make this head one whit funnier:

ROBS POLICE CHIEF OF GUN

What shall be said of puns? Despite all the scoffing to which the punster is subjected, the pun unquestionably has its place in humor. It therefore also has its place in the headline. But a pun that would be bad anywhere else does not achieve respectability by being set in 24-point type in a headline. Rather it works the other way around. The pun becomes the worse for its very conspicuousness. Any examples here would be superfluous. The merits of a pun are too much a matter of taste.

Appropriateness, we have noted, is the keynote of the humorous head, as well as of all feature heads. One illustration should suffice to indicate what is meant. Here is the lead of a story that was written in light style:

OSSINING, N.Y., Nov. 22—Taking advantage of the trustfulness of Alabama Pitts and his Sing Sing prison football team the Port Jervis Police Department slipped thirteen "ringers" in against the convict eleven at the prison field today and won a victory by proxy. The score was Sing Sing 0, Port Jervis 13.

The story features not only the very situation of a playful encounter between police and convicts but also the incongruity that lies in the "cheating" of innocent, trusting prisoners by the supposedly upright representatives of the law. Note how the headline catches the spirit of this:

POLICE ROB SING SING
OF A FOOTBALL GAME

The Pathetic Story. Little need be said about stories of pathos, for once again matters of taste are involved. The same principles of restraint that apply to the writing of the story apply to the writing of the head; it should be neither too "sobby" nor maudlin. Here, for once, the brevity necessitated in the headline is usually advantageous, because it makes for dignified understatement and hence effectiveness. And, once more, the head should be keyed to the spirit of the article. Incidentally, in this kind of story as also in the romanticized story, the copy editor should guard against characterization by such words as "heroic" or "pitiful" or "great exploit" or "tragedy." The facts should be set forth; they will speak for themselves.

Thus ends the discussion of headline technique. We have examined the headline to discover what it is and have delved somewhat into its history. We have described its appearance and learned how to dress it in becoming clothes, we have studied how it conveys its message clearly, quickly, accurately and attractively and we have examined the code of usage that has grown up designed to make it fulfill its functions with the greatest effectiveness.

The aim of all this has not been to bring about a dull standardization in headline writing. If there is one outstanding fault in present day headlines, it is that very sameness with which they speak, day in and day out. Much of this monotony is inevitable because of the cramping space limitation that compels repeated use of words, phrases and constructions that have been found most serviceable. This limitation is one of the copy editor's chief discouragements, but at the same time it adds zest to his work and makes victory for originality the more glorious.

No, the intention has not been to produce standardization, but rather to set up ideal standards, in so far as this is possible—not standards that will inhibit the copy editor's work, but standards that will serve as a measure of its effectiveness. This is the most that can be done. There is, after all, no substitute for intelligence and skill, which are indispensable in this difficult business of headlining.

10. A CLINIC FOR AILING HEADLINES

JUST AS the classroom work of the student doctor becomes real when he is confronted with an actual patient, so the student of copy editing may be helped if he is confronted at this point with a group of actual headlines that demonstrate assorted ailments.

A good many of these patients, but not all, exhibit a common symptom—ambiguity. Others suffer from obscurity. There is a remedy for both ambiguity and obscurity, but it is not easy to apply. The copy editor must summon to mind the fact that whereas the story is known to him since he has just read it, it is not known to the newspaper reader. The copy editor therefore must figuratively pull back from the headline he has just written and try to view it afresh, as if he were a reader seeing it for the first time. He must determine whether it will instantly convey meaning to the reader or whether it is just a jumble of words. This treatment will help to cure obscurity. The copy editor must also examine every word and phrase in the head to see whether it is susceptible of a meaning different from the one intended, and in so doing he must assume the reader to be a really perverse fellow. This treatment will help to cure ambiguity. It cannot be overemphasized that if the headline is to serve its purpose it must be clear at first glance.

Let us examine a dozen categories of sick headlines:

1. *Two-faced heads*. (Double meanings.)

DIVER GETS CROSS
IN ICY RIVER RITE

Why wouldn't he?

U.S. RULES ON TAX
ADOPTED BY STATE

Is "rules" a noun or a verb?

YOUTH OF 80 LANDS
AT RALLY IN INDIA

"Lands" is intended to be a noun, but that is not instantly clear.

LANDLADY ADMITS
SIXTY VIOLATIONS

No comment necessary.

2. *Deadheads*. (They say nothing.)

PROSECUTION RESTS

What trial is being referred to?

SUPPORT IS REAFFIRMED

Deadheads are produced by lazy or overhasty editors. The cure for this headline malady is simply the injunction set forth in a previous chapter: Be specific. At the very least the headline must contain some word or phrase that identifies the subject matter of the story.

3. *Heads that say too much*. (They go beyond the facts or overstate them.)

JUDGE SUGGESTS JAIL
FOR UNWED MOTHERS

In the story what the judge suggested was that unwed mothers of three or more children be jailed. He was not proposing to penalize all unwed mothers, as the head suggests, but rather was taking the view that anyone could make a mistake—or two.

PLEVEN TO FORM
CABINET IN PARIS

M. Pleven agreed to try to form a cabinet. The head goes too far in saying flatly that he is going to form one. Actually in this instance the head was proved wrong within forty-eight hours. He failed.

4. *Misleading heads.* (They give a wrong impression.)

RUSSIAN BLOWS
UP AIRLINER

The story said that a Russian who suddenly went berserk exploded a hand grenade aboard a Venezuelan plane causing it to crash. Thus, the head makes no incorrect statement. Still the use of the word "Russian," particularly at a time when the Russians were being troublesome to the West, suggests a story quite different from the one that would be suggested by the word "madman," for instance. Deliberately or inadvertently, the head is misleading. This is as bad as if it had been incorrect.

250 FLEE FIRE IN SHIP

Fire at Sea? No. It was a forest fire and 250 were evacuated from the area in a small craft.

5. *Faultily constructed heads.* (Words or phrases out of place.)

NEW DATA FOUND
ON MRS. LINCOLN

Sounds as if she was frisked.

PANACEAS SCORED
FOR DELINQUENCY

What are delinquent panaceas?

SOLDIER SAVES AIRLINER

Lights Army Strip for Plane
Without Any Electricity

It is not immediately clear whether "without any electricity" applies to "lights" or to "plane."

6. *Heads containing ambiguous words.* (Two-faced heads with a special problem.)

LEGISLATOR HURT
IN CRASH IS GRAVE

Some adjectives describing a person's state of health are ambiguous. Here are two headlines that appeared in a single issue of a newspaper:

QUEENS MAN STILL CRITICAL
CANDIDATE IS CRITICAL

The first reported the aftermath of a fall, the second reported a political speech. Some adjectives of this kind are unambiguous—"healthy," "well," "ill," "sick." Others could be ambiguous but usually are not—"better," "improved," "worse." Still others can be, and often are, ambiguous, and these are the ones to watch out for—"grave," "critical," "serious," "fine," "good" and "satisfactory." They should never appear in heads unattended by "condition" or "health" or "doctors find" or something else that dissipates any possible misunderstanding.

7. *Noun-instead-of-adjective heads.*

POLAND WORKERS
SHUT DOWN DOCKS

Since "Polish" would fit in this head, the use of "Poland" is inexcusable. The use of nouns as adjectives is a normal occurrence in English and should not be ruled out of headlines, as was explained in a previous chapter. But when nouns are used abnormally, as "Poland" is in this headline, the usage is disapproved.

8. *Incompletely worded heads.* (Words omitted willy-nilly.)

CULTURAL INSTITUTIONS FEARED LEAVING
MORNINGSIDE IF HOUSING STILL LAGS

Although it is permissible in headlines to omit nonessential words, it must be possible by supplying the missing words to obtain a normal, grammatical English sentence. This is not possible in the quoted head.

9. *Vague heads.* (Too remote from subject.)

ARMS COLLECTOR
DEFENDS OBJECT

This head seems to be about a connoisseur of weapons, a notion that is reinforced by the word "object," which suggests *objet d'art*. In reality the story was about a man charged with establishing an arsenal for the Irish Republican Army, who was defending the goal of his action. The headline writer knew what the story was, but how was the poor reader to guess?

10. *Split heads.* (Otherwise known as wrap-around heads.)

NIXON AGAIN DECLARES U.S.
MIGHT COULD DETER ATTACK

Normally the split head does not lead to this much discomfort. Here it lends momentary ambiguity to the word "might."

11. *Rhymed heads.* (They're oh so pat and fall so flat.)

'POET IN WAITING'
BIDS FOR A RATING

The story was about Robert Frost, who assuredly was not given to jingles of that sort. The copy editor might as well make up his mind to it: In trying to achieve poetry in the limited confines of a headline the best he is ever likely to get is doggerel. If that is appropriate (see page 163), fine. Otherwise, no.

Here is a tabloid head that escapes the mediocrity of a mere jingle and would pass—in any tabloid:

MADCAP MAYOR
JAILED, BAILED
AND UNQUAILED

12. Punning heads. (With double-play words.)

PITCHER HAD A FINE SERIES

This was about a baseball player who was fined for unbecoming behavior in the world series.

GIANTS GET BOOT OUT OF CHANDLER

About a punter on the Giants football team. Both heads are very funny, no? No.

Two tests can be propounded for puns, whether in a headline or elsewhere. The first is whether each of the two meanings of the word forming the pun is appropriate. A rather fair pun that meets this test is included in the following head on a story about high school youths who visited shops to study merchandising:

STUDENTS LEARN
WHAT'S IN STORE

The second test is based on the theory that the basis of humor is incongruity and unexpectedness. This means that the pun should not be obvious; it should not be just lying around waiting to be picked up, as it was in each of the first two heads quoted.

Puns that don't come off can be very sad indeed, as the examples show. The best advice that can be given to the headline writer is to avoid the pun unless he is convinced that it is exceptionally good. If there is one thing that most newspapers need, it is more sophistication. The bad pun, like the childish rhyme, is the mortal enemy of this quality.

11. A HEADLINE VOCABULARY OF RELATED WORDS

ONE overwhelming advantage that the experienced headline writer has over the novice is facility in calling to mind synonyms and substitute words when one word is unserviceable because of its length or because of an incorrect shade of meaning. This facility, of course, depends to some extent on the vocabulary of the worker, but to a much larger extent it is the result of practice. Whereas the beginner might fumble for a word for many minutes, the veteran can usually summon one almost instantaneously.

The list of the most common headline words presented herewith was assembled in an attempt to offset in part this handicap. But, in addition, it is hoped that the list will prove valuable to the experienced desk man in speeding up his work and in helping him over those tortuous moments when the required word mischievously eludes him.

A danger that seemed apparent when the idea for this list was conceived was that it would make for undesirable standardization of expression, that it would cause the headline writer to imitate rather than to create. To avoid this as far as possible, the list deliberately excludes all phrases and figures of speech, so that it will not suggest hackneyed headline constructions.

The list is made up of main entries and cross references in simple alphabetical order. Each main entry is a key word and is followed by a group of related words. It should be emphasized that the list is in no sense a dictionary of synonyms, as it includes more than mere synonyms and at the same time disregards those that have no headline utility. Furthermore, words are grouped solely on the basis of the headline ideas they suggest, sometimes making strange but not uncongenial bedfellows.

The main entry, or key word, does not, and is not intended to cover all the meanings of the words in that particular grouping. It is purely arbitrary and was chosen simply because of the general thought it suggests.

An asterisk following a word indicates that the word is viewed with disfavor for headline purposes and would better be avoided altogether or used sparingly.

A

abandon: *see* RESIGN
abandonment: *see* RESIGN
abate: *see* FALL; STOP
abatement: *see* FALL; STOP
abdicate: *see* RESIGN
abdication: *see* RESIGN
abduct: *see* DISAPPEAR
abduction: *see* DISAPPEAR
abet: *see* APPROVAL
abolish: *see* RELIEVE; STOP
abolition: *see* RELIEVE; STOP
absolve: *see* ACQUIT
absorb: *see* ORGANIZATION
ACCIDENT
   Verbs
  collide
  crash
  crush
  hit
  ram
  smash
  strike
   Nouns
  catastrophe
  collision
  crash
  disaster
  mishap
  smash-up
  tragedy
  wreck
acclaim: *see* APPROVAL
accord: *see* GIVE; PEACE
ACCUSE: *see also* OPPOSITION
   Verbs
  allege
  arraign
  ascribe
  attribute
  blame
  charge
  cite

ACCUSE (*cont.*)
credit
denounce
implicate
indict
involve
lay
link
name
  Nouns
allegation
blame
charge
denunciation
indictment
true bill
acknowledge: *see* ADMIT
acknowledgment: *see* ADMIT
acme: *see* PEAK
acquire: *see* GET
acquisition: *see* GET
ACQUIT
  Verbs
absolve
clear
defend
exonerate
free
release
uphold
vindicate
  Nouns
acquittal
exoneration
freedom
release
vindication
acquittal: *see* ACQUIT
act: *see* ADVANCE; ORDER; START
action: *see* ADVANCE
add: *see* RISE
addition: *see* RISE
address: *see* SAY
adjust: *see* REVISE
adjustment: *see* REVISE
admission: *see* ADMIT

ADMIT
  Verbs
acknowledge
avow
concede
confess
own
  Nouns
acknowledgment
admission
avowal
confession
adopt: *see* APPROVAL
adoption: *see* APPROVAL
ADVANCE
  Verbs
act
bring
cause
expedite
facilitate
hasten
impel
press
prod
push
quicken
result
rush
speed
spur
stimulate
stir
  Nouns
action
progress
speed
adversary: *see* OPPOSITION
affect: *see* DAMAGE
affirm: *see* SAY
affirmation: *see* SAY
afford: *see* GIVE
agenda: *see* PLAN
agree: *see* PEACE; PLAN; PROMISE
agreement: *see* PEACE; PLAN; PROM-
  ISE

aid: *see* APPROVAL; RELIEVE
aim: *see* PLAN
alarm: *see* DANGER
allay: *see* RELIEVE
allegation: *see* ACCUSE; SAY
allege: *see* ACCUSE; SAY
alleviate: *see* RELIEVE
alleviation: *see* RELIEVE
alliance: *see* ORGANIZATION
allocate: *see* GIVE
allocation: *see* GIVE
allot: *see* GIVE
allotment: *see* GIVE
allow: *see* APPROVAL
ally: *see* ORGANIZATION
alter: *see* REVISE
alteration: *see* REVISE
amaze: *see* PUZZLE
amazement: *see* PUZZLE
amend: *see* REVISE
amendment: *see* REVISE
amity: *see* PEACE
analysis: *see* INVESTIGATE
analyze: *see* INVESTIGATE
anger: *see* ANNOY
angry: *see* ANNOY
announce: *see* SHOW
announcement: *see* SHOW
ANNOY: *see also* RIDICULE
   Verbs
  anger
  arouse
  awaken
  bother
  disturb
  enrage
  fret
  harass
  harry
  irk
  irritate
  stir
  torment
  vex
   Nouns
  anger

  disturbance
  fury
  ire
  rage
  wrath
   Adjectives
  angry
  irate
  wroth
answer: *see* REPLY
anticipate: *see* PREDICT
anticipation: *see* PREDICT
anxiety: *see* DANGER
anxious: *see* DANGER
apartment: *see* BUILDING
apathetic: *see* CALM
apathy: *see* CALM
appeal: *see* REQUEST
applaud: *see* APPROVAL
appoint: *see* CHOOSE
appointment: *see* CHOOSE
apportion: *see* GIVE
apportionment: *see* GIVE
apprehend: *see* ARREST
approach: *see* FACE
APPROVAL: *see also* ADVANCE
   Verbs
  abet
  acclaim
  adopt
  aid
  allow
  applaud
  approve
  ask
  assist
  authorize
  back
  commend
  confirm
  defend
  demand
  encourage
  endorse
  espouse
  eulogize

APPROVAL (*cont.*)
extol
favor
further
gratify
hail
hearten
help
justify
laud
pass
permit
please
propose
ratify
request
sanction
seek
suggest
support
sustain
uphold
urge
vote
want
   Nouns
acclaim
adoption
aid
assistance
authorization
backing
commendation
confirmation
defense
endorsement
eulogy
favor
help
passage
permission
plaudit
ratification
sanction
support

approve: *see* APPROVAL
arbitrate: *see* PEACE
arbitration: *see* PEACE
ARDENT
    Nouns
ardor
avidity
cordiality
eagerness
enthusiasm
fervor
joy
zeal
    Adjectives
avid
cordial
eager
enthusiastic
fervent
joyful
zealous
ardor: *see* ARDENT
AREA
    Nouns
district
locality
neighborhood
place
region
scene
section
site
sphere
tract
vicinity
zone
argue: *see* DISCUSS; OPPOSITION
argument: *see* DISCUSS; OPPOSITION
arise: *see* RISE
armistice: *see* PEACE
arouse: *see* ANNOY
arraign: *see* ACCUSE
arrange: *see* PLAN
arrangement: *see* PEACE; PLAN
array: *see* MEETING

ARREST
   Verbs
apprehend
capture
catch
hold
net
round up
seize
take
trap
   Nouns
apprehension
capture
roundup
seizure
ascend: *see* RISE
ascension: *see* RISE
ascent: *see* RISE
ascribe: *see* ACCUSE
ask: *see* APPROVAL; QUESTION; RE-
  QUEST
aspersion: *see* BELITTLE
assail: *see* OPPOSITION
assault: *see* OPPOSITION
assemblage: *see* MEETING
assemble: *see* MEETING
assembly: *see* MEETING
assert: *see* SAY
assertion: *see* SAY
assess: *see* TAX
assessment: *see* TAX
assist: *see* APPROVAL
assistance: *see* APPROVAL
association: *see* ORGANIZATION
assurance: *see* PROMISE
assure: *see* PROMISE
astonish: *see* PUZZLE
astonishment: *see* PUZZLE
astound: *see* PUZZLE
attack: *see* OPPOSITION
attitude: *see* POLICY
attribute: *see* ACCUSE
augment: *see* RISE
authority: *see* LEADER

authorization: *see* APPROVAL
authorize: *see* APPROVAL
aver: *see* SAY
avert: *see* STOP
avid: *see* ARDENT
avidity: *see* ARDENT
avoid: *see* STOP
avow: *see* ADMIT; SAY
avowal: *see* ADMIT; PROMISE; SAY
awaken: *see* ANNOY
await: *see* FACE
award: *see* GIVE; ORDER
awe: *see* PUZZLE

B

back: *see* APPROVAL
backing: *see* APPROVAL
baffle: *see* PUZZLE
bake: *see* HEAT
balk: *see* PUZZLE; STOP
ban: *see* OPPOSITION; STOP
band: *see* ORGANIZATION
bandit: *see* STEAL
bar: *see* OPPOSITION; STOP
bare: *see* SHOW
bargain: *see* PEACE
barrier: *see* STOP
batter: *see* STORM
battle: *see* OPPOSITION; VIO-
  LENCE
beat: *see* WIN
beg: *see* REQUEST
begin: *see* START
beginning: *see* START
belief: *see* POLICY; SAY
believe: *see* SAY
BELITTLE: *see also* RIDICULE
   Verbs
deprecate
depreciate
discount
discredit
disparage
disregard

BELITTLE (*cont.*)
  ignore
  malign
  minimize
  shun
  slight
  slur
  spurn
  undermine
    Nouns
  aspersion
  disparagement
  slight
  slur
bequeath: *see* GIVE
bequest: *see* GIVE
berate: *see* OPPOSITION
beseech: *see* REQUEST
best: *see* WIN
bestow: *see* GIVE
bestowal: *see* GIVE
betray: *see* SHOW
better: *see* RELIEVE
betterment: *see* RELIEVE
bewilder: *see* PUZZLE
bewilderment: *see* PUZZLE
BIAS
    Verbs
  discriminate
  favor
  prejudice
    Nouns
  discrimination
  favoritism
  leaning
  prejudice
    Adjectives
  partial
  unfair
bicker: *see* OPPOSITION
bid: *see* ORDER; REQUEST
blame: *see* ACCUSE
blanket: *see* SNOW
blast: *see* COLD
blaze: *see* FIRE

blizzard: *see* SNOW; STORM
block: *see* STOP
blow: *see* OPPOSITION
board: *see* ORGANIZATION
body: *see* ORGANIZATION
bolt: *see* ESCAPE; STORM
bond: *see* ORGANIZATION
boo: *see* RIDICULE
booty: *see* STEAL
bother: *see* ANNOY
bow: *see* LOSE
branch: *see* ORGANIZATION
brand: *see* DESCRIBE
brave: *see* DANGER
brawl: *see* VIOLENCE
breach: *see* OPPOSITION
break: *see* ESCAPE; OPPOSITION;
  STORM
bring: *see* ADVANCE
broaden: *see* RISE
buffet: *see* STORM
build: *see* BUILDING
BUILDING
    Verbs
  build
  construct
  erect
  rear
  rise
    Nouns
  apartment
  center
  edifice
  house
  institution
  plant
  skyscraper
  structure
  tenement
  tower
burden: *see* DIFFICULTY; TAX
burglar: *see* STEAL
burglary: *see* STEAL
burn: *see* FIRE
bury: *see* HIDE; SNOW

C

cache: *see* HIDE
call: *see* DESCRIBE
call for: *see* REQUEST
CALM: *see also* PEACE
   Verbs
  hush
  quiet
  silence
  soothe
  still
   Nouns
  apathy
  coolness
  indifference
  inertia
  neutrality
  quiet
  torpor
  unconcern
   Adjectives
  apathetic
  cold
  cool
  firm
  indifferent
  mum*
  mute
  neutral
  quiet
  silent
  unconcerned
  unmoved
CAMPAIGN: *see also* OPPOSITION
   Nouns
  course
  drive
  effort
  move
  program
cancel: *see* OPPOSITION
cap: *see* PEAK
capture: *see* ARREST
catastrophe: *see* ACCIDENT

catcall: *see* RIDICULE
catch: *see* ARREST
catechize: *see* QUESTION
cause: *see* ADVANCE
caution: *see* DANGER
cease: *see* STOP
cede: *see* GIVE
celebrate: *see* CEREMONY
celebration: *see* CEREMONY
censure: *see* OPPOSITION
center: *see* BUILDING;
  ORGANIZATION
CEREMONY
   Verbs
  celebrate
  hold
  mark
  observe
  perform
  stage
   Nouns
  celebration
  display
  event
  exercises
  fete
  observance
  pageant
  parade
  party
  performance
  procession
  review
  service
  spectacle
chairman: *see* LEADER
challenge: *see* OPPOSITION; QUES-
  TION
change: *see* REVISE
chaos: *see* VIOLENCE
charge: *see* ACCUSE; ORDER; SAY
chart: *see* PLAN
chase: *see* PURSUE
chat: *see* SAY
cheat: *see* STEAL

check: see STOP
cheer: see GREET; HONOR
chide: see OPPOSITION; RIDICULE
chief: see LEADER
chill: see COLD
choice: see CHOOSE
choke: see SNOW; STOP
CHOOSE
   Verbs
  appoint
  designate
  elect
  name
  nominate
  pick
  select
   Nouns
  appointment
  choice
  designation
  election
  nomination
  selection
cite: see ACCUSE; SAY
claim: see SAY
clamor: see VIOLENCE
clash: see OPPOSITION; VIOLENCE
clear: see ACQUIT
climax: see PEAK
climb: see RISE
cloak: see HIDE; SNOW
clog: see SNOW; STOP
close: see STOP
closing: see STOP
cloudburst: see STORM
club: see ORGANIZATION
clue: see DISCOVER
COLD: see *also* CALM
   Verbs
  chill
  freeze
  grip
  nip
  sweep
   Nouns
  blast

  chill
  mercury
  spell
  temperature
  thermometer
  wave
   Adjectives
  chill
  frigid
  icy
  wintry
collapse: see FALL
collide: see ACCIDENT
collision: see ACCIDENT
combat: see OPPOSITION; VIOLENCE
combination: see ORGANIZATION
combine: see ORGANIZATION
command: see LEADER; ORDER
commander: see LEADER
commence: see START
commend: see APPROVAL
commendation: see APPROVAL
commission: see ORGANIZATION
committee: see ORGANIZATION
compact: see PEACE
company: see ORGANIZATION
COMPARE
   Verbs
  contrast
  liken
  link
  parallel
   Nouns
  comparison
  contrast
  likeness
  parallel
comparison: see COMPARE
complete: see STOP
completion: see STOP
conceal: see HIDE
concede: see ADMIT
concern: see DANGER; ORGANIZATION
conciliate: see PEACE
conciliation: see PEACE
concord: see PEACE

condemn: *see* OPPOSITION
condemnation: *see* OPPOSITION
confer: *see* GIVE; MEETING
conference: *see* MEETING
confess: *see* ADMIT
confession: *see* ADMIT
confirm: *see* APPROVAL
confirmation: *see* APPROVAL
conflagration: *see* FIRE
conflict: *see* OPPOSITION; VIOLENCE
confound: *see* PUZZLE
confront: *see* FACE
confuse: *see* PUZZLE
confusion: *see* PUZZLE; VIOLENCE
congratulate: *see* HONOR
congratulation: *see* HONOR
congregate: *see* MEETING
congress: *see* MEETING
conquer: *see* WIN
consider: *see* DISCUSS; SAY
consolidate: *see* ORGANIZATION
conspiracy: *see* PLAN
conspire: *see* PLAN
construct: *see* BUILDING
contend: *see* SAY
contention: *see* SAY
contest: *see* OPPOSITION
contradict: *see* DENY
contradiction: *see* DENY
contrast: *see* COMPARE
contribute: *see* GIVE
contribution: *see* GIVE
control: *see* LEADER; ORDER
controversy: *see* OPPOSITION
convene: *see* MEETING
convention: *see* MEETING
convocation: *see* MEETING
convoke: *see* MEETING
cool: *see* CALM
coolness: *see* CALM
cordial: *see* ARDENT
cordiality: *see* ARDENT
corporation: *see* ORGANIZATION
corps: *see* ORGANIZATION
correct: *see* RELIEVE
correction: *see* RELIEVE

corrective: *see* RELIEVE
course: *see* CAMPAIGN
cover: *see* FLOOD; SNOW
cow: *see* STOP
crash: *see* ACCIDENT
create: *see* START
creation: *see* START
credit: *see* ACCUSE
crest: *see* PEAK
cripple: *see* DAMAGE; STOP
crown: *see* PEAK
crush: *see* ACCIDENT; WIN
curb: *see* STOP
cure: *see* RELIEVE
curtail: *see* STOP
curtailment: *see* STOP
custom: *see* TAX
cut: *see* FALL
cyclone: *see* STORM

D

DAMAGE
  Verbs
  affect
  cripple
  destroy
  gut*
  harm
  hurt
  impair
  injure
  level
  mar
  ravage
  raze
  ruin
  scar
  spoil
  wreck
  Nouns
  debris
  destruction
  harm
  hurt
  injury

DAMAGE (*cont.*)
  loss
  ruin
  wreckage
DANGER
  Verbs
  brave
  caution
  concern
  dare
  defend
  dread
  endanger
  fear
  frighten
  guard
  imperil
  jeopardize
  menace
  peril
  protect
  risk
  scent
  terrify
  terrorize
  threaten
  trouble
  warn
  Nouns
  alarm
  anxiety
  caution
  concern
  fear
  flurry
  fright
  hazard
  jeopardy
  menace
  peril
  risk
  scare*
  tension
  terror
  threat
  trouble

  Adjectives
  anxious
  tense
  wary
dare: *see* DANGER
deadlock: *see* STOP
deal: *see* PEACE
DEATH
  Verbs
  destroy
  die
  execute
  kill
  murder
  perish
  slay
  succumb
  Nouns
  destruction
  execution
  homicide
  killing
  manslaughter
  murder
  slaughter
  slaying
  suicide
debate: *see* DISCUSS; OPPOSITION
debris: *see* DAMAGE
deceive: *see* STEAL
decide: *see* PLAN; SAY
decision: *see* ORDER
declaration: *see* SAY
declare: *see* SAY
decline: *see* FALL
decrease: *see* FALL
decree: *see* ORDER
decry: *see* OPPOSITION
deem: *see* SAY
defalcate: *see* STEAL
defalcation: *see* STEAL
defeat: *see* LOSE; WIN
defend: *see* ACQUIT; APPROVAL; DAN-
  GER
defense: *see* APPROVAL
defer: *see* POSTPONE

defiance: *see* OPPOSITION
deflate: *see* FALL
deflation: *see* FALL
defraud: *see* STEAL
defy: *see* OPPOSITION
delay: *see* POSTPONE
deluge: *see* FLOOD; STORM
delve: *see* INVESTIGATE
demand: *see* APPROVAL; REQUEST
demonstrate: *see* SHOW; VIOLENCE
demonstration: *see* SHOW; VIOLENCE
denial: *see* DENY
denounce: *see* ACCUSE; OPPOSITION
denunciation: *see* ACCUSE; OPPOSI-
   TION
DENY
   Verbs
   contradict
   disavow
   disclaim
   disown
   dispute
   gainsay
   recant
   refuse
   refute
   reject
   renounce
   repudiate
   retract
   scout
   withhold
   Nouns
   contradiction
   denial
   disavowal
   disclaimer
   refusal
   refutation
   rejection
   renunciation
   repudiation
   retraction
depart: *see* DISAPPEAR
depict: *see* DESCRIBE
deplore: *see* OPPOSITION

depose: *see* RESIGN
deprecate: *see* BELITTLE
depreciate: *see* BELITTLE
depress: *see* FALL
depression: *see* FALL
deride: *see* RIDICULE
derision: *see* RIDICULE
descend: *see* FALL
descent: *see* FALL
DESCRIBE
   Verbs
   brand
   call
   depict
   explain
   name
   narrate
   outline
   picture
   portray
   relate
   report
   style
   tell
   term
   Nouns
   description
   explanation
   narrative
   outline
   portrayal
   report
   story
   tale
description: *see* DESCRIBE
desert: *see* RESIGN
desertion: *see* RESIGN
design: *see* PLAN
designate: *see* CHOOSE
designation: *see* CHOOSE
desire: *see* REQUEST
destroy: *see* DAMAGE; DEATH
destruction: *see* DAMAGE; DEATH
detect: *see* DISCOVER
detection: *see* DISCOVER
deter: *see* STOP

determine: *see* DISCOVER; PLAN
develop: *see* ORGANIZATION; RISE
dictate: *see* LEADER; ORDER
dictator: *see* LEADER
die: *see* DEATH
differ: *see* OPPOSITION
DIFFICULTY
    Nouns
  burden
  distress
  evil
  ill
  malady
  onus
  trouble
  woe
dig up: *see* DISCOVER
dim: *see* DISAPPEAR
diminish: *see* FALL
din: *see* VIOLENCE
direct: *see* LEADER; ORDER
director: *see* LEADER
disagree: *see* OPPOSITION
DISAPPEAR
    Verbs
  abduct
  depart
  dim
  elope
  fade
  go
  kidnap
  leave
  lose
  melt
  quit
  vanish
    Nouns
  abduction
  disappearance
  kidnapping
  loss
  runaway
    Adjectives
  gone
  missing

disappearance: *see* DISAPPEAR
disapproval: *see* OPPOSITION
disapprove: *see* OPPOSITION
disaster: *see* ACCIDENT
disavow: *see* DENY
disavowal: *see* DENY
discard: *see* OPPOSITION
discern: *see* DISCOVER; SAY
disclaim: *see* DENY
disclaimer: *see* DENY
disclose: *see* SHOW
disclosure: *see* SHOW
discord: *see* OPPOSITION; VIOLENCE
discount: *see* BELITTLE
DISCOVER: *see also* SHOW
    Verbs
  detect
  determine
  dig up
  discern
  ferret
  find
  solve
  unearth
  unravel
    Nouns
  clue
  detection
  discovery
  find
  key
  lead
  solution
discovery: *see* DISCOVER
discredit: *see* BELITTLE
discriminate: *see* BIAS
discrimination: *see* BIAS
DISCUSS
    Verbs
  argue
  consider
  debate
  take up
  weigh
    Nouns
  argument

DISCUSS (*cont.*)
   debate
   discussion
   forum
   symposium
discussion: *see* DISCUSS
dislike: *see* OPPOSITION
dismiss: *see* RESIGN
dismissal: *see* RESIGN
disorder: *see* VIOLENCE
disown: *see* DENY
disparage: *see* BELITTLE
disparagement: *see* BELITTLE
display: *see* CEREMONY; SHOW
dispute: *see* DENY; OPPOSITION
disregard: *see* BELITTLE
dissension: *see* OPPOSITION
dissent: *see* OPPOSITION
distress: *see* DIFFICULTY
distribute: *see* GIVE
distribution: *see* GIVE
district: *see* AREA
disturb: *see* ANNOY
disturbance: *see* ANNOY;
   VIOLENCE
dive: *see* FALL
divide: *see* OPPOSITION
division: *see* OPPOSITION
divulge: *see* SHOW
dodge: *see* ESCAPE
donate: *see* GIVE
donation: *see* GIVE
doubt: *see* QUESTION
doubtful: *see* QUESTION
down: *see* FALL; WIN
downpour: *see* STORM
draft: *see* PLAN
draw: *see* PLAN
drawing: *see* PLAN
dread: *see* DANGER
drive: *see* CAMPAIGN
drop: *see* FALL
dubious: *see* QUESTION
due: *see* PREDICT
dupe: *see* STEAL
duplicity: *see* STEAL

duty: *see* TAX
dwindle: *see* FALL

E

eager: *see* ARDENT
eagerness: *see* ARDENT
earn: *see* GET
earthquake: *see* SHAKE
ease: *see* RELIEVE
ebb: *see* FALL
edict: *see* ORDER
edifice: *see* BUILDING
effort: *see* CAMPAIGN
elect: *see* CHOOSE
election: *see* CHOOSE
electrify: *see* PUZZLE
elope: *see* DISAPPEAR
elude: *see* ESCAPE
embezzle: *see* STEAL
embezzlement: *see* STEAL
emit: *see* GIVE
encourage: *see* APPROVAL
end: *see* RELIEVE; STOP
endanger: *see* DANGER
endorse: *see* APPROVAL
endorsement: *see* APPROVAL
endow: *see* GIVE
endowment: *see* GIVE
enemy: *see* OPPOSITION
enhance: *see* RISE
enjoin: *see* ORDER; STOP
enlarge: *see* RISE
enrage: *see* ANNOY
enter: *see* START
enterprise: *see* PLAN
enthusiasm: *see* ARDENT
enthusiastic: *see* ARDENT
entreat: *see* REQUEST
entreaty: *see* REQUEST
envisage: *see* PREDICT
erect: *see* BUILDING
ESCAPE: *see also* DISAPPEAR
   Verbs
   bolt
   break

ESCAPE (*cont.*)
  dodge
  elude
  evade
  flee
  get away
  make off
    Nouns
  bolt
  break
  evasion
  flight
  getaway
  runaway
eschew: *see* OPPOSITION
espouse: *see* APPROVAL
eulogize: *see* APPROVAL; HONOR
eulogy: *see* APPROVAL; HONOR
evade: *see* ESCAPE
evasion: *see* ESCAPE
event: *see* CEREMONY
evidence: *see* SHOW
evil: *see* DIFFICULTY
evince: *see* SHOW
exact: *see* TAX
exaction: *see* TAX
exalt: *see* HONOR
examination: *see* INVESTIGATE
examine: *see* INVESTIGATE
exceed: *see* RISE
excel: *see* WIN
excise: *see* TAX
execute: *see* DEATH
execution: *see* DEATH
exercises: *see* CEREMONY
exhibit: *see* SHOW
exhibition: *see* SHOW
exhort: *see* REQUEST
exonerate: *see* ACQUIT
exoneration: *see* ACQUIT
expand: *see* RISE
expansion: *see* RISE
expect: *see* FACE; PLAN; PREDICT
expectation: *see* PREDICT
expedite: *see* ADVANCE
expedition: *see* PURSUE

expel: *see* RESIGN
experiment: *see* SHOW
expert: *see* LEADER
explain: *see* DESCRIBE; SAY
explanation: *see* DESCRIBE; SAY
exposé: *see* SHOW
exposition: *see* SHOW
expound: *see* SAY
expulsion: *see* RESIGN
extend: *see* RISE
extension: *see* RISE
extol: *see* APPROVAL; HONOR
extort: *see* STEAL
extortion: *see* STEAL

F

FACE
    Verbs
  approach
  await
  confront
  expect
  impend
  look for
  loom
  near
  prepare
  wait
    Adjectives
  imminent
  liable
  near
  poised
  ready
facilitate: *see* ADVANCE
fade: *see* DISAPPEAR
fail: *see* FALL; LOSE; STOP
failure: *see* LOSE
FALL
    Verbs
  abate
  collapse
  cut
  decline
  decrease

FALL (*cont.*)
  deflate
  depress
  descend
  diminish
  dive
  drop
  dwindle
  ebb
  fail
  lessen
  narrow
  pare
  plunge
  prune
  recede
  reduce
  sag
  shave
  sink
  slash
  slump
  trim
  tumble
  wane
    Nouns
  abatement
  collapse
  cut
  decline
  decrease
  deflation
  depression
  descent
  dive
  drop
  ebb
  plunge
  recede
  reduction
  slash
  slump
    Adverbs
  down
  low
  off

fashion: *see* ORGANIZATION; PLAN
favor: *see* APPROVAL; BIAS
favoritism: *see* BIAS
fear: *see* DANGER
feel: *see* SAY
felicitate: *see* HONOR
felicitation: *see* HONOR
ferret: *see* DISCOVER
fervent: *see* ARDENT
fervor: *see* ARDENT
fete: *see* CEREMONY
fight: *see* OPPOSITION; VIOLENCE
filibuster: *see* STOP
final: *see* STOP
finale: *see* STOP
find: *see* DISCOVER; SAY
finish: *see* STOP
FIRE
    Verbs
  blaze
  burn
  flame
  flare
  ignite
    Nouns
  blaze
  conflagration
  flames
  holocaust
firm: *see* CALM; ORGANIZATION
first: *see* START
fix: *see* PLAN
flame: *see* FIRE
flames: *see* FIRE
flare: *see* FIRE; RISE
flay*: *see* OPPOSITION
flee: *see* ESCAPE
fleece: *see* STEAL
flight: *see* ESCAPE
FLOOD
    Verbs
  cover
  deluge
  inundate
  submerge
  wash

FLOOD (*cont.*)
   Nouns
  inundation
  overflow
  torrent
flout: *see* OPPOSITION
flurry: *see* DANGER
foe: *see* OPPOSITION
foil: *see* STOP
follow: *see* PURSUE
forbid: *see* STOP
forecast: *see* PREDICT
foresee: *see* PREDICT
forestall: *see* STOP
foretell: *see* PREDICT
form: *see* ORGANIZATION
forum: *see* DISCUSS; MEETING
found: *see* START
fracas: *see* VIOLENCE
frame: *see* PLAN
fraud: *see* STEAL
fray: *see* VIOLENCE
free: *see* ACQUIT; RELIEVE
freedom: *see* ACQUIT
freeze: *see* COLD
fret: *see* ANNOY
fright: *see* DANGER
frighten: *see* DANGER
frigid: *see* COLD
frown: *see* OPPOSITION
fruitless: *see* LOSE
frustrate: *see* STOP
frustration: *see* STOP
furor: *see* VIOLENCE
further: *see* APPROVAL
fury: *see* ANNOY; VIOLENCE
futile: *see* LOSE

G

gain: *see* RISE; GET
gainsay: *see* DENY
gale: *see* STORM
game: *see* OPPOSITION
gang: *see* ORGANIZATION
gather: *see* MEETING
gathering: *see* MEETING

GET: *see also* STEAL
   Verbs
  acquire
  earn
  gain
  obtain
  receive
  win
   Nouns
  acquisition
getaway: *see* ESCAPE
gibe: *see* RIDICULE
gift: *see* GIVE
GIVE
   Verbs
  accord
  afford
  allocate
  allot
  apportion
  bequeath
  bestow
  cede
  confer
  contribute
  distribute
  donate
  emit
  endow
  grant
  hand
  issue
  leave
  offer
  pay
  present
  provide
  share
  submit
  vent
  will
  yield
   Nouns
  allocation
  allotment
  apportionment
  award

GIVE (*cont.*)
  bequest
  bestowal
  contribution
  distribution
  donation
  endowment
  gift
  grant
  legacy
  offer
  payment
  present
  provision
give in: *see* LOSE
give up: *see* LOSE
give way: *see* LOSE
go: *see* DISAPPEAR
gone: *see* DISAPPEAR
grant: *see* GIVE
gratify: *see* APPROVAL
GREET: *see also* CEREMONY
    Verbs
  cheer
  hail
  meet
  receive
  salute
  welcome
    Nouns
  greeting
  reception
  welcome
greeting: *see* GREET
grip: *see* COLD; STORM
group: *see* ORGANIZATION
grow: *see* RISE
growth: *see* RISE
guard: *see* DANGER; HIDE
guide: *see* LEADER
guild: *see* ORGANIZATION
gut*: *see* DAMAGE

H

hail: *see* APPROVAL; GREET; HONOR
halt: *see* STOP

hand: *see* GIVE
harass: *see* ANNOY
harm: *see* DAMAGE
harmonize: *see* PEACE
harmony: *see* PEACE
harry: *see* ANNOY; PURSUE
hasten: *see* ADVANCE
hazard: *see* DANGER
head: *see* LEADER
heal: *see* PEACE
hearten: *see* APPROVAL
HEAT
    Verbs
  bake
  oppress
  sizzle
  stifle
  swelter
    Nouns
  mercury
  temperature
  thermometer
  spell
  wave
    Adjectives
  humid
  oppressive
  stifling
  sultry
  torrid
height: *see* PEAK
heighten: *see* RISE
help: *see* APPROVAL; RELIEVE
HIDE: *see also* ESCAPE
    Verbs
  bury
  cache
  cloak
  conceal
  guard
  mask
  screen
  secrete
  veil
  withhold
    Nouns
  cache

HIDE (*cont.*)
  cloak
  mask
  screen
  veil
higher: *see* RISE
hinder: *see* STOP
hindrance: *see* STOP
hint: *see* SAY
hiss: *see* RIDICULE
hit: *see* ACCIDENT; OPPOSITION
hitch: *see* STOP
hold: *see* ARREST; CEREMONY; SAY
hold up: *see* STEAL; STOP
holdup: *see* STEAL
holocaust: *see* FIRE
homage: *see* HONOR
homicide: *see* DEATH
HONOR: *see also* CEREMONY; GREET
  Verbs
  cheer
  congratulate
  eulogize
  exalt
  extol
  felicitate
  hail
  lionize
  revere
  Nouns
  congratulation
  eulogy
  felicitation
  homage
  reverence
  tribute
hoot: *see* RIDICULE
hope: *see* PREDICT
hound: *see* PURSUE
house: *see* BUILDING;
  ORGANIZATION
howl: *see* STORM
humble: *see* WIN
humid: *see* HEAT
hunt: *see* PURSUE
hurricane: *see* STORM

hurt: *see* DAMAGE
hush: *see* CALM

I

icy: *see* COLD
idea: *see* PLAN
ignite: *see* FIRE
ignore: *see* BELITTLE
ill: *see* DIFFICULTY
imminent: *see* FACE
impair: *see* DAMAGE
impart: *see* SHOW
impede: *see* STOP
impel: *see* ADVANCE
impend: *see* FACE
imperil: *see* DANGER
impetus: *see* START
implicate: *see* ACCUSE
implore: *see* REQUEST
impose: *see* TAX
impost: *see* TAX
imprison: *see* STOP
improve: *see* RELIEVE
improvement: *see* RELIEVE
inaugurate: *see* START
inauguration: *see* START
inception: *see* START
increase: *see* RISE
indicate: *see* PREDICT; SHOW
indication: *see* PREDICT; SHOW
indict: *see* ACCUSE
indictment: *see* ACCUSE
indifference: *see* CALM
indifferent: *see* CALM
induct: *see* START
induction: *see* START
inertia: *see* CALM
inflate: *see* RISE
inflation: *see* RISE
influence: *see* LEADER
initial: *see* START
initiate: *see* START
injunction: *see* ORDER; STOP
injure: *see* DAMAGE
injury: *see* DAMAGE

inquire: *see* INVESTIGATE; QUESTION
inquiry: *see* INVESTIGATE; QUESTION
insist: *see* SAY
install: *see* START
installation: *see* START
institute: *see* MEETING; START
institution: *see* BUILDING;
    ORGANIZATION
intend: *see* PREDICT
intention: *see* PREDICT
interfere: *see* STOP
interference: *see* STOP
interrogate: *see* QUESTION
interrogation: *see* QUESTION
interrupt: *see* STOP
interruption: *see* STOP
intimate: *see* SAY
intimation: *see* SAY
inundate: *see* FLOOD
inundation: *see* FLOOD
INVESTIGATE
    Verbs
    analyze
    delve
    examine
    inquire
    plumb
    probe*
    pry*
    scan
    scrutinize
    sift*
    sound
    study
    Nouns
    analysis
    examination
    inquiry
    probe*
    scrutiny
    study
invitation: *see* REQUEST
invite: *see* REQUEST
invoke: *see* REQUEST
involve: *see* ACCUSE
irate: *see* ANNOY

ire: *see* ANNOY
irk: *see* ANNOY
irritate: *see* ANNOY
issue: *see* GIVE; POLICY; SHOW

J

jam: *see* STOP
jar: *see* SHAKE
jeer: *see* RIDICULE
jeopardize: *see* DANGER
jeopardy: *see* DANGER
jest: *see* RIDICULE
join: *see* ORGANIZATION
joke: *see* RIDICULE
jolt: *see* SHAKE
joy: *see* ARDENT
joyful: *see* ARDENT
jump: *see* RISE
justify: *see* APPROVAL

K

key: *see* DISCOVER
kidnap: *see* DISAPPEAR
kidnapping: *see* DISAPPEAR
kill: *see* DEATH
killing: *see* DEATH
knit: *see* ORGANIZATION

L

larceny: *see* STEAL
lash: *see* OPPOSITION; STORM
last: *see* STOP
latest: *see* STOP
laud: *see* APPROVAL
laugh: *see* RIDICULE
laughter: *see* RIDICULE
law: *see* ORDER
lay: *see* ACCUSE
lead: *see* DISCOVER; LEADER; WIN
LEADER
    Verbs
    command
    control
    dictate

LEADER (*cont.*)
  direct
  guide
  head
  influence
  lead
  persuade
  reign
  rule
  sway
    Nouns
  authority
  chairman
  chief
  command
  commander
  control
  dictator
  director
  expert
  head
  notable
  pioneer
  president
  regime
  reign
  rule
  ruler
leaning: *see* BIAS
leave: *see* DISAPPEAR; GIVE; RESIGN
legacy: *see* GIVE
lessen: *see* FALL
letup: *see* RELIEVE
level: *see* DAMAGE
levy: *see* TAX
liable: *see* FACE
lift: *see* RELIEVE; RISE
lighten: *see* RELIEVE
likelihood: *see* PREDICT
likely: *see* PREDICT
liken: *see* COMPARE
likeness: *see* COMPARE
limit: *see* STOP
link: *see* ACCUSE; COMPARE;
  ORGANIZATION
lionize: *see* HONOR

list: *see* SHOW
load: *see* TAX
locality: *see* AREA
lock: *see* STOP
look for: *see* FACE
loom: *see* FACE
loosen: *see* RELIEVE
loot: *see* STEAL
LOSE: *see also* DISAPPEAR
    Verbs
  bow
  fail
  give in
  give up
  give way
  submit
  succumb
  surrender
  yield
    Nouns
  defeat
  failure
  loss
  setback
  surrender
    Adjectives
  fruitless
  futile
  vain
loss: *see* DAMAGE; DISAPPEAR; LOSE
low: *see* FALL

M

maintain: *see* SAY
make off: *see* ESCAPE
malady: *see* DIFFICULTY
malign: *see* BELITTLE
manslaughter: *see* DEATH
mantle: *see* SNOW
map: *see* PLAN
mar: *see* DAMAGE
mark: *see* CEREMONY
marshal: *see* MEETING
mask: *see* HIDE
master: *see* WIN

match: *see* OPPOSITION
measure: *see* ORDER
meet: *see* GREET; MEETING; REPLY
MEETING
  Verbs
 array
 assemble
 confer
 congregate
 convene
 convoke
 gather
 marshal
 meet
 mobilize
 rally
 reunite
 unite
  Nouns
 assemblage
 assembly
 conference
 congress
 convention
 convocation
 forum
 gathering
 institute
 parley
 rally
 reunion
 session
 talk(s)
melee: *see* VIOLENCE
melt: *see* DISAPPEAR
menace: *see* DANGER
mercury: *see* COLD; HEAT
merge: *see* ORGANIZATION
merger: *see* ORGANIZATION
minimize: *see* BELITTLE
mishap: *see* ACCIDENT
missing: *see* DISAPPEAR
mitigate: *see* RELIEVE
mix-up: *see* VIOLENCE
mobilize: *see* MEETING
mock: *see* RIDICULE

mockery: *see* RIDICULE
modification: *see* REVISE
modify: *see* REVISE
mount: *see* RISE
move: *see* CAMPAIGN; START
muddle: *see* PUZZLE
mum*: *see* CALM
murder: *see* DEATH
mute: *see* CALM
mutiny: *see* VIOLENCE
mystery: *see* PUZZLE
mystify: *see* PUZZLE

N

name: *see* ACCUSE; CHOOSE; DE-
  SCRIBE
narrate: *see* DESCRIBE
narrative: *see* DESCRIBE
narrow: *see* FALL
near: *see* FACE
neighborhood: *see* AREA
net: *see* ARREST
neutral: *see* CALM
neutrality: *see* CALM
nip: *see* COLD
noise: *see* VIOLENCE
nominate: *see* CHOOSE
nomination: *see* CHOOSE
nonplus: *see* PUZZLE
notable: *see* LEADER
nullify: *see* OPPOSITION

O

oath: *see* PROMISE
observance: *see* CEREMONY
observe: *see* CEREMONY
obstacle: *see* STOP
obstruct: *see* STOP
obstruction: *see* STOP
obtain: *see* GET
off: *see* FALL
offer: *see* GIVE
onslaught: *see* OPPOSITION
onus: *see* DIFFICULTY
open: *see* START

opening: *see* START
opinion: *see* ORDER
oppose: *see* OPPOSITION
OPPOSITION: *see also* BELITTLE; STOP
 Verbs
 argue
 assail
 attack
 ban
 bar
 battle
 berate
 bicker
 break
 cancel
 censure
 challenge
 chide
 clash
 combat
 condemn
 conflict
 contest
 debate
 decry
 defy
 denounce
 deplore
 differ
 disagree
 disapprove
 discard
 dislike
 dispute
 dissent
 divide
 eschew
 fight
 flay*
 flout
 frown
 hit*
 lash
 nullify
 outlaw
 pit*

protest
quarrel
rap
rebuff
rebuke
reject
repel
reproach
reprove
repudiate
rule out
slap*
split
upbraid
veto
vie
void
war
 Nouns
adversary
argument
assault
attack
battle
blow
breach
break
censure
challenge
clash
combat
condemnation
conflict
contest
controversy
defiance
denunciation
disapproval
discord
dislike
dispute
dissension
dissent
division
enemy
fight

OPPOSITION (*cont.*)
 foe
 game
 match
 onslaught
 protest
 quarrel
 rebuff
 rebuke
 reproach
 rift
 rival
 row
 schism
 split
 strife
 struggle
 tilt*
 tournament
 war
oppress: *see* HEAT
oppressive: *see* HEAT
ORDER
  Verbs
 bid
 charge
 command
 control
 decree
 dictate
 direct
 enjoin
 prescribe
 rule
 tell
  Nouns
 act
 award
 command
 control
 decision
 decree
 edict
 injunction
 law
 measure

 opinion
 ordinance
 rule
 ruling
 statute
 ukase*
 verdict
 writ
ordinance: *see* ORDER
ORGANIZATION
  Verbs
 absorb
 ally
 band
 combine
 consolidate
 develop
 fashion
 form
 join
 knit
 link
 merge
 pool
 shape
 tie
 unite
 weld
  Nouns
 alliance
 association
 band
 board
 body
 bond
 branch
 center
 club
 combination
 combine*
 commission
 committee
 company
 concern
 corporation
 corps

ORGANIZATION (*cont.*)
  firm
  gang
  group
  guild
  house
  institution
  merger
  party
  pool
  racket
  ring
  society
  syndicate
  tie
  union
  unit
organize: *see* ORGANIZATION
oust: *see* RESIGN
ouster: *see* RESIGN
outlaw: *see* OPPOSITION; STEAL
outline: *see* DESCRIBE; PLAN
outlook: *see* PREDICT
overcome: *see* WIN
overflow: *see* FLOOD
overwhelm: *see* WIN
own: *see* ADMIT

P

pacify: *see* PEACE
pact: *see* PEACE
pageant: *see* CEREMONY
panacea: *see* RELIEVE
panic: *see* VIOLENCE
parade: *see* CEREMONY
parallel: *see* COMPARE
paralyze: *see* STOP
pare: *see* FALL
parley: *see* MEETING
partial: *see* BIAS
party: *see* CEREMONY; ORGANIZATION
pass: *see* APPROVAL
passage: *see* APPROVAL
patch: *see* PEACE

pause: *see* STOP
pay: *see* GIVE
payment: *see* GIVE
PEACE
    Verbs
  agree
  arbitrate
  conciliate
  harmonize
  heal
  pacify
  patch
  placate
  reconcile
  settle
  smooth
    Nouns
  accord
  agreement
  amity
  arbitration
  armistice
  arrangement
  bargain
  compact
  conciliation
  concord
  deal
  harmony
  pact*
  settlement
  transaction
  treaty
  truce
PEAK
    Verbs
  cap
  climax
  crown
  top
    Nouns
  acme
  cap
  climax
  crest

PEAK (*cont.*)
  crown
  height
  top
perceive: *see* PREDICT
perfect: *see* PLAN
perform: *see* CEREMONY
performance: *see* CEREMONY
peril: *see* DANGER
perish: *see* DEATH
permission: *see* APPROVAL
permit: *see* APPROVAL
perplex: *see* PUZZLE
persuade: *see* LEADER
pick: *see* CHOOSE
picture: *see* DESCRIBE
pigeonhole: *see* POSTPONE
pioneer: *see* LEADER
pit: *see* OPPOSITION
placate: *see* PEACE; RELIEVE
place: *see* AREA
PLAN
    Verbs
  agree
  aim
  arrange
  conspire
  decide
  design
  determine
  draft
  draw
  expect
  fashion
  fix
  frame
  map
  outline
  perfect
  plot
  polish
  prepare
  project
  propose
  scheme

  set
  shape
  sketch
  suggest
    Nouns
  agenda
  agreement
  aim
  arrangement
  chart
  conspiracy
  design
  drawing
  enterprise
  idea
  outline
  plot
  program
  project
  proposal
  scheme
  sketch
  suggestion
  undertaking
plank: *see* POLICY
plant: *see* BUILDING
platform: *see* POLICY
plaudit: *see* APPROVAL
plea: *see* REQUEST
plead: *see* REQUEST
please: *see* APPROVAL
pledge: *see* PROMISE
plot: *see* PLAN
plumb: *see* INVESTIGATE
plunder: *see* STEAL
plunge: *see* FALL
poised: *see* FACE
POLICY
    Nouns
  attitude
  belief
  issue
  plank
  platform
  stand

POLICY (*cont.*)
  subject
  topic
  view
polish: *see* PLAN
pool: *see* ORGANIZATION
portray: *see* DESCRIBE
portrayal: *see* DESCRIBE
posse: *see* PURSUE
possibility: *see* PREDICT
possible: *see* PREDICT
POSTPONE: *see also* STOP
    Verbs
  defer
  delay
  pigeonhole
  prolong
  put off
  shelve
  table
    Nouns
  delay
  postponement
postponement: *see* POSTPONE
pound: *see* STORM
pray: *see* REQUEST
prayer: *see* REQUEST
PREDICT: *see also* FACE
    Verbs
  anticipate
  envisage
  expect
  forecast
  foresee
  foretell
  hope
  indicate
  intend
  perceive
  prophesy
  scent
  schedule
  see
  slate
  vision
  warn

    Nouns
  anticipation
  expectation
  forecast
  hope
  indication
  intention
  likelihood
  outlook
  possibility
  prediction
  probability
  prophecy
  vision
  warning
    Adjectives
  due
  likely
  possible
  probable
prediction: *see* PREDICT
prejudice: *see* BIAS
prepare: *see* FACE; PLAN
prescribe: *see* ORDER
present: *see* GIVE
president: *see* LEADER
press: *see* ADVANCE
prevail: *see* WIN
prevent: *see* STOP
primary: *see* START
probability: *see* PREDICT
probable: *see* PREDICT
probe*: *see* INVESTIGATE
procession: *see* CEREMONY
proclaim: *see* SAY
prod: *see* ADVANCE
program: *see* CAMPAIGN; PLAN
progress: *see* ADVANCE
prohibit: *see* STOP
prohibition: *see* STOP
project: *see* PLAN
prolong: *see* POSTPONE
PROMISE: *see also* PEACE
    Verbs
  agree
  assure

PROMISE (*cont.*)
  pledge
  swear
  vow
   Nouns
  agreement
  assurance
  avowal
  oath
  pledge
  vow
prophecy: *see* PREDICT
prophesy: *see* PREDICT
proposal: *see* PLAN
propose: *see* APPROVAL; PLAN
protect: *see* DANGER
protest: *see* OPPOSITION
provide: *see* GIVE
provision: *see* GIVE
prune: *see* FALL
pry*: *see* INVESTIGATE
publish: *see* SHOW
PURSUE
   Verbs
  chase
  follow
  harry
  hound
  hunt
  search
  seek
  trace
  track
  trail
   Nouns
  chase
  expedition
  hunt
  posse
  pursuit
  quarry
  quest
  search
  trace
  track
  trail

pursuit: *see* PURSUE
push: *see* ADVANCE
put off: *see* POSTPONE
PUZZLE
   Verbs
  amaze
  astonish
  astound
  awe
  baffle
  balk
  bewilder
  confound
  confuse
  electrify
  mystify
  nonplus
  perplex
  shock
  stagger
  startle
  stun
  surprise
   Nouns
  amazement
  astonishment
  awe
  bewilderment
  confusion
  muddle
  mystery
  shock
  snarl
  surprise
  tangle

Q

quake: *see* SHAKE
quarrel: *see* OPPOSITION
quarry: *see* PURSUE
quell: *see* STOP
query: *see* QUESTION
quest: *see* PURSUE
QUESTION: *see also* INVESTIGATE
   Verbs
  ask

QUESTION (*cont.*)
  catechize
  challenge
  doubt
  inquire
  interrogate
  query
  quiz*
    Nouns
  challenge
  doubt
  inquiry
  interrogation
  query
    Adjectives
  doubtful
  dubious
quicken: *see* ADVANCE
quiet: *see* CALM
quit: *see* DISAPPEAR; RESIGN
quiver: *see* SHAKE
quiz*: *see* QUESTION
quotation: *see* SAY
quote: *see* SAY

R

racket: *see* ORGANIZATION; STEAL
racketeer: *see* STEAL
rage: *see* ANNOY; STORM
raid: *see* STEAL
rally: *see* MEETING
ram: *see* ACCIDENT
ransack: *see* STEAL
rap*: *see* OPPOSITION
ratification: *see* APPROVAL
ratify: *see* APPROVAL
ravage: *see* DAMAGE
raze: *see* DAMAGE
ready: *see* FACE
realign: *see* REVISE
realignment: *see* REVISE
rear: *see* BUILDING
rebel: *see* VIOLENCE
rebellion: *see* VIOLENCE
rebuff: *see* OPPOSITION
rebuke: *see* OPPOSITION

rebuttal: *see* REPLY
recant: *see* DENY
recede: *see* FALL
receive: *see* GET; GREET; MEETING
reception: *see* GREET
reconcile: *see* PEACE
record: *see* SHOW
rectify: *see* RELIEVE
reduce: *see* FALL
reduction: *see* FALL
reform: *see* RELIEVE
refusal: *see* DENY
refuse: *see* DENY
refutation: *see* DENY; REPLY
refute: *see* DENY; REPLY
regard: *see* SAY
regime: *see* LEADER
region: *see* AREA
register: *see* SHOW
reign: *see* LEADER
reject: *see* DENY; OPPOSITION
rejection: *see* DENY
rejoinder: *see* REPLY
relate: *see* DESCRIBE
relax: *see* RELIEVE
release: *see* ACQUIT
relief: *see* RELIEVE
RELIEVE: *see also* APPROVAL
    Verbs
  abolish
  aid
  allay
  alleviate
  better
  correct
  cure
  ease
  end
  free
  help
  improve
  lift
  lighten
  loosen
  mitigate
  placate
  rectify

RELIEVE (*cont.*)
  reform
  relax
  remedy
  repair
  rescue
  rid
  save
  slacken
  soften
  succor
  temper
    Nouns
  abolition
  aid
  alleviation
  betterment
  correction
  corrective
  cure
  end
  help
  improvement
  letup
  panacea
  reform
  relief
  remedy
  rescue
  succor
remedy: *see* RELIEVE
renounce: *see* DENY
renunciation: *see* DENY
repair: *see* RELIEVE
repel: *see* OPPOSITION; STOP
REPLY: *see also* DENY
    Verbs
  answer
  meet
  refute
  respond
  retort
    Nouns
  answer
  rebuttal
  refutation
  rejoinder

  response
  retort
report: *see* DESCRIBE
repress: *see* STOP
repression: *see* STOP
reproach: *see* OPPOSITION
reproof: *see* OPPOSITION
reprove: *see* OPPOSITION
repudiate: *see* DENY; OPPOSITION
repudiation: *see* DENY
repulse: *see* STOP; WIN
repulsion: *see* STOP
REQUEST: *see also* APPROVAL
    Verbs
  appeal
  ask
  beg
  beseech
  bid
  call for
  demand
  desire
  entreat
  exhort
  implore
  invite
  invoke
  plead
  pray
  seek
  solicit
  urge
  want
    Nouns
  appeal
  demand
  desire
  entreaty
  invitation
  plea
  prayer
rescue: *see* RELIEVE
RESIGN
    Verbs
  abandon
  abdicate
  depose

RESIGN (*cont.*)
  desert
  dismiss
  expel
  leave
  oust
  quit
  retire
    Nouns
  abandonment
  abdication
  desertion
  dismissal
  expulsion
  leave
  ouster
  resignation
  retirement
resignation: *see* RESIGN
respond: *see* REPLY
response: *see* REPLY
restrain: *see* STOP
restraint: *see* STOP
restrict: *see* STOP
restriction: *see* STOP
result: *see* ADVANCE
retard: *see* STOP
retire: *see* RESIGN
retirement: *see* RESIGN
retort: *see* REPLY
retract: *see* DENY
retraction: *see* DENY
reunion: *see* MEETING
reunite: *see* MEETING
reveal: *see* SHOW
revelation: *see* SHOW
revenue: *see* TAX
revere: *see* HONOR
reverence: *see* HONOR
review: *see* CEREMONY
REVISE
    Verbs
  adjust
  alter
  amend
  change

  modify
  realign
  shake up
  shift
  switch
  transfer
  transform
  vary
    Nouns
  adjustment
  alteration
  amendment
  change
  modification
  realignment
  revision
  shake-up
  shift
  switch
  transformation
  variation
revision: *see* REVISE
revolt: *see* VIOLENCE
revolution: *see* VIOLENCE
rid: *see* RELIEVE
RIDICULE: *see also* OPPOSITION
    Verbs
  boo
  chide
  deride
  gibe
  hiss
  hoot
  insult
  jeer
  jest
  joke
  laugh
  mock
  scoff
  scorn
  scout
  sneer
  taunt
  tease
  twit

RIDICULE (*cont.*)
    Nouns
  boo
  catcall
  derision
  gibe
  hiss
  hoot
  insult
  jeer
  jest
  joke
  laughter
  mockery
  scorn
  sneer
  taunt
rifle: *see* STEAL
rift: *see* OPPOSITION
ring: *see* ORGANIZATION
riot: *see* VIOLENCE
RISE: *see also* BUILDING
    Verbs
  add
  arise
  ascend
  augment
  broaden
  climb
  develop
  enhance
  enlarge
  exceed
  expand
  extend
  flare
  gain
  grow
  heighten
  increase
  inflate
  jump
  lift
  mount
  skyrocket
  soar

  surpass
  swell
  tower
  wax
  widen
    Nouns
  addition
  ascension
  ascent
  climb
  expansion
  extension
  gain
  growth
  increase
  inflation
  jump
    Adverbs
  higher
  up
risk: *see* DANGER
rival: *see* OPPOSITION
rob: *see* STEAL
robbery: *see* STEAL
rock: *see* SHAKE
round up: *see* ARREST
roundup: *see* ARREST
rout: *see* WIN
row: *see* OPPOSITION; VIOLENCE
ruin: *see* DAMAGE
rule: *see* SAY; LEADER; ORDER
rule out: *see* OPPOSITION
ruler: *see* LEADER
ruling: *see* ORDER
runaway: *see* DISAPPEAR; ESCAPE
ruse: *see* STEAL
rush: *see* ADVANCE

S

sag: *see* FALL
salute: *see* GREET
sanction: *see* APPROVAL
save: *see* RELIEVE
SAY
    Verbs
  address

SAY (*cont.*)
  affirm
  allege
  assert
  aver*
  avow
  believe
  charge
  chat
  cite
  claim*
  consider
  contend
  decide
  declare
  deem
  discern
  explain
  expound
  feel
  find
  hint
  hold
  insist
  intimate
  maintain
  proclaim
  quote
  regard
  rule
  see
  speak
  state*
  suggest
  swear
  talk
  tell
  testify
  think
  utter
  view
  voice
    Nouns
  address
  affirmation
  allegation

assertion
avowal
belief
charge
chat
claim
contention
declaration
explanation
hint
intimation
quotation
speech
statement
suggestion
talk
testimony
utterance
view
scan: *see* INVESTIGATE
scare*: *see* DANGER
scene: *see* AREA
scent: *see* DANGER; PREDICT
schedule: *see* PREDICT
scheme: *see* PLAN
schism: *see* OPPOSITION
scoff: *see* RIDICULE
score: *see* WIN
scorn: *see* RIDICULE
scout: *see* DENY; RIDICULE
screen: *see* HIDE
scrutinize: *see* INVESTIGATE
scrutiny: *see* INVESTIGATE
search: *see* PURSUE
secrete: *see* HIDE
section: *see* AREA
see: *see* PREDICT; SAY
seek: *see* APPROVAL; PURSUE; RE-
  QUEST
seize: *see* ARREST; STEAL
seizure: *see* ARREST
select: *see* CHOOSE
selection: *see* CHOOSE
service: *see* CEREMONY
session: *see* MEETING
set: *see* PLAN

setback: *see* LOSE
settle: *see* PEACE
settlement: *see* PEACE
set up: *see* START
SHAKE
   Verbs
jar
jolt
quake
quiver
rock
shock
totter
tremble
upset
   Nouns
earthquake
jar
jolt
quake
quiver
shock
temblor*
tremor
upset
shake up: *see* REVISE
shake-up: *see* REVISE
shape: *see* ORGANIZATION; PLAN
share: *see* GIVE
shave: *see* FALL
shelve: *see* POSTPONE
shift: *see* REVISE
shock: *see* PUZZLE; SHAKE
SHOW
   Verbs
announce
bare
betray
demonstrate
disclose
display
divulge
evince
exhibit
experiment
expose

impart
indicate
issue
list
publish
record
register
reveal
sound
test
try
uncover
unfold
   Nouns
announcement
demonstration
disclosure
display
evidence
exhibit
exhibition
experiment
exposé
exposition
indication
record
revelation
test
trial
shun: *see* BELITTLE
sift*: *see* INVESTIGATE
silence: *see* CALM
silent: *see* CALM
sink: *see* FALL
site: *see* AREA
sizzle: *see* HEAT
sketch: *see* PLAN
skyrocket: *see* RISE
skyscraper: *see* BUILDING
slacken: *see* RELIEVE; STOP
slap*: *see* OPPOSITION
slash: *see* FALL
slate: *see* PREDICT
slaughter: *see* DEATH
slay: *see* DEATH
slaying: *see* DEATH

slight: *see* BELITTLE
slow: *see* STOP
slump: *see* FALL
slur: *see* BELITTLE
smash: *see* ACCIDENT; STORM
smash-up: *see* ACCIDENT
smooth: *see* PEACE
snag: *see* STOP
snarl: *see* PUZZLE; STOP
sneer: *see* RIDICULE
SNOW: *see also* COLD; STORM
   Verbs
  blanket
  bury
  choke
  cloak
  clog
  cover
  fall
  mantle
   Nouns
  blanket
  blizzard
  cloak
  fall
  mantle
  storm
soar: *see* RISE
society: *see* ORGANIZATION
soften: *see* RELIEVE
solicit: *see* REQUEST
solution: *see* DISCOVER
solve: *see* DISCOVER
sound: *see* INVESTIGATE; SHOW
speak: *see* SAY
spectacle: *see* CEREMONY
speech: *see* SAY
speed: *see* ADVANCE
spell: *see* COLD; HEAT
sphere: *see* AREA
split: *see* OPPOSITION
spoil: *see* DAMAGE
spur: *see* ADVANCE
spurn: *see* BELITTLE
stage: *see* CEREMONY
stagger: *see* PUZZLE

stall: *see* STOP
stampede: *see* VIOLENCE
stand: *see* POLICY
START
   Verbs
  act
  begin
  commence
  create
  enter
  found
  inaugurate
  induct
  initiate
  install
  institute
  move
  open
  set up
   Nouns
  beginning
  creation
  impetus
  inauguration
  inception
  induction
  installation
  move
  opening
   Adjectives
  first
  initial
  primary
startle: *see* PUZZLE
state: *see* SAY
statement: *see* SAY
statute: *see* ORDER
stay: *see* STOP
STEAL
   Verbs
  cheat
  deceive
  defalcate
  defraud
  dupe
  embezzle

STEAL (*cont.*)
 extort
 fleece
 get
 hold up
 loot
 plunder
 raid
 ransack
 rifle
 rob
 seize
 swindle
 take
 trick
 wrest
  Nouns
 bandit
 booty
 burglar
 burglary
 defalcation
 duplicity
 embezzlement
 extortion
 fraud
 holdup
 larceny
 loot
 outlaw
 plunder
 racket
 racketeer
 raid
 robbery
 ruse
 swindle
 theft
 thief
 thug
 trick
stem: *see* STOP
stifle: *see* HEAT
stifling: *see* HEAT
still: *see* CALM
stimulate: *see* ADVANCE

stir: *see* ADVANCE; ANNOY
STOP: *see also* OPPOSITION
  Verbs
 abate
 abolish
 avert
 avoid
 balk
 ban
 bar
 block
 cease
 check
 choke
 clog
 close
 complete
 cow
 cripple
 curb
 curtail
 deadlock
 deter
 end
 enjoin
 fail
 filibuster
 finish
 foil
 forbid
 forestall
 frustrate
 halt
 hinder
 impede
 imprison
 interfere
 interrupt
 jam
 limit
 lock
 obstruct
 paralyze
 pause
 prevent
 prohibit

STOP (*cont.*)
quell
repel
repress
repulse
restrain
restrict
retard
slacken
slow
snag
snarl
stall
stay
stem
suppress
suspend
tangle
terminate
thwart
tie up
Nouns
abatement
abolition
ban
bar
barrier
check
closing
completion
curb
curtailment
deadlock
end
filibuster
finale
finish
halt
hindrance
hitch
injunction
interference
interruption
jam
limit
obstacle

obstruction
pause
prohibition
repression
restraint
restriction
snag
snarl
stay
suppression
suspension
tangle
tie-up
Adjectives
complete
final
last
latest

STORM: *see also* COLD; DAMAGE;
FLOOD; SNOW
Verbs
batter
break
buffet
grip
howl
lash
pound
rage
smash
strike
sweep
toss
whirl
whistle
Nouns
blizzard
bolt
cloudburst
cyclone
deluge
downpour
gale
hurricane
tempest
tornado

STORM (*cont.*)
  twister
  wind
story: *see* DESCRIBE
strife: *see* OPPOSITION
strike: *see* ACCIDENT; STORM
structure: *see* BUILDING
struggle: *see* OPPOSITION; VIOLENCE
study: *see* INVESTIGATE
stun: *see* PUZZLE
style: *see* DESCRIBE
subdue: *see* WIN
subject: *see* POLICY
submerge: *see* FLOOD
submit: *see* GIVE; LOSE
succeed: *see* WIN
success: *see* WIN
succor: *see* RELIEVE
succumb: *see* DEATH; LOSE
suggest: *see* APPROVAL; PLAN; SAY
suggestion: *see* PLAN; SAY
suicide: *see* DEATH
sultry: *see* HEAT
support: *see* APPROVAL
suppress: *see* STOP
suppression: *see* STOP
surpass: *see* RISE
surprise: *see* PUZZLE
surrender: *see* LOSE
suspend: *see* STOP
suspension: *see* STOP
sustain: *see* APPROVAL
swamp: *see* WIN
sway: *see* LEADER
swear: *see* PROMISE; SAY
sweep: *see* COLD; STORM; WIN
swell; *see* RISE
swelter: *see* HEAT
swindle: *see* STEAL
switch: *see* REVISE
symposium: *see* DISCUSS
syndicate: *see* ORGANIZATION

T

table: *see* POSTPONE
take: *see* ARREST; STEAL

take up: *see* DISCUSS
tale: *see* DESCRIBE
talk: *see* SAY
talk(s): *see* MEETING
tangle: *see* PUZZLE; STOP
tariff: *see* TAX
taunt: *see* RIDICULE
TAX
    Verbs
  assess
  burden
  exact
  impose
  levy
    Nouns
  assessment
  burden
  custom
  duty
  exaction
  excise
  impost
  levy
  load
  revenue
  tariff
  toll
tease: *see* RIDICULE
tell: *see* DESCRIBE; ORDER; SAY
temblor*: *see* SHAKE
temper: *see* RELIEVE
temperature: *see* COLD; HEAT
tempest: *see* STORM
tenement: *see* BUILDING
tense: *see* DANGER
tension: *see* DANGER
term: *see* DESCRIBE
terminate: *see* STOP
terrify: *see* DANGER
terror: *see* DANGER
terrorize: *see* DANGER
test: *see* SHOW
testify: *see* SAY
testimony: *see* SAY
theft: *see* STEAL
thermometer: *see* COLD; HEAT

thief: see STEAL
think: see DANGER
threat: see DANGER
threaten: see DANGER
thug: see STEAL
thwart: see STOP
tie: see ORGANIZATION
tie up: see STOP
tie-up: see STOP
tilt*: see OPPOSITION
toll: see TAX
top: see PEAK; WIN
topic: see POLICY
torment: see ANNOY
tornado: see STORM
torpor: see CALM
torrent: see FLOOD
torrid: see HEAT
toss: see STORM
totter: see SHAKE
tournament: see OPPOSITION
tower: see BUILDING; RISE
trace: see PURSUE
track: see PURSUE
tract: see AREA
tragedy: see ACCIDENT
trail: see PURSUE
transaction: see PEACE
transfer: see REVISE
transform: see REVISE
transformation: see REVISE
trap: see ARREST
treaty: see PEACE
tremble: see SHAKE
tremor: see SHAKE
trial: see SHOW
tribute: see HONOR
trick: see STEAL
trim: see FALL
triumph: see WIN
trouble: see DANGER; DIFFICULTY;
    VIOLENCE
truce: see PEACE
true bill: see ACCUSE
try: see SHOW
tumble: see FALL

tumult: see VIOLENCE
turmoil: see VIOLENCE
twister: see STORM
twit: see RIDICULE

U

ukase*: see ORDER
unconcern: see CALM
unconcerned: see CALM
uncover: see SHOW
undermine: see BELITTLE
undertaking: see PLAN
unearth: see DISCOVER
unfair: see BIAS
unfold: see SHOW
union: see ORGANIZATION
unit: see ORGANIZATION
unite: see MEETING; ORGANIZATION
unmoved: see CALM
unravel: see DISCOVER
up: see RISE
upbraid: see OPPOSITION
uphold: see ACQUIT; APPROVAL
uprising: see VIOLENCE
uproar: see VIOLENCE
upset: see SHAKE
urge: see APPROVAL; REQUEST
utter: see SAY
utterance: see SAY

V

vain: see LOSE
vanish: see DISAPPEAR
vanquish: see WIN
variation: see REVISE
vary: see REVISE
veil: see HIDE
vent: see GIVE
verdict: see ORDER
veto: see OPPOSITION
vex: see ANNOY
vicinity: see AREA
victor: see WIN
victory: see WIN
vie: see OPPOSITION

view: *see* POLICY; SAY
vindicate: *see* ACQUIT
vindication: *see* ACQUIT
VIOLENCE: *see also* OPPOSITION
    Verbs
  battle
  brawl
  clamor
  clash
  combat
  demonstrate
  fight
  mutiny
  rebel
  revolt
  riot
  stampede
  struggle
    Nouns
  battle
  brawl
  chaos
  clamor
  clash
  combat
  conflict
  confusion
  demonstration
  din
  discord
  disorder
  disturbance
  fight
  fracas
  fray
  fury
  furor
  melee
  mix-up
  mutiny
  noise
  panic
  rebellion
  revolt
  riot
  row

  stampede
  struggle
  trouble
  tumult
  turmoil
  uprising
  uproar
vision: *see* PREDICT
voice: *see* SAY
void: *see* OPPOSITION
vote: *see* APPROVAL
vow: *see* PROMISE

W

wait: *see* FACE
wane: *see* FALL
want: *see* APPROVAL; REQUEST
war: *see* OPPOSITION
warn: *see* DANGER; PREDICT
warning: *see* PREDICT
wary: *see* DANGER
wash: *see* FLOOD
wave: *see* COLD: HEAT
wax: *see* RISE
weigh: *see* DISCUSS
welcome: *see* GREET
weld: *see* ORGANIZATION
whirl: *see* STORM
whistle: *see* STORM
widen: *see* RISE
will: *see* GIVE
WIN: *see also* GET
    Verbs
  beat
  best
  better
  conquer
  crush
  defeat
  down
  excel
  gain
  humble
  lead
  master

WIN (*cont.*)
  overcome
  overwhelm
  prevail
  repulse
  rout
  score
  subdue
  succeed
  swamp
  sweep
  top
  triumph
  vanquish
    Nouns
  lead
  master
  rout
  success
  sweep
  triumph

  victor
  victory
wind: *see* STORM
wintry: *see* COLD
withhold: *see* DENY; HIDE
woe: *see* DIFFICULTY
wrath: *see* ANNOY
wreck: *see* ACCIDENT; DAMAGE
wreckage: *see* DAMAGE
wrest: *see* STEAL
writ: *see* ORDER
wroth: *see* ANNOY

Y

yield: *see* GIVE; LOSE

Z

zeal: *see* ARDENT
zealous: *see* ARDENT
zone: *see* AREA

A GLOSSARY OF NEWSPAPER TERMS

NOTE: TERMS FOR BOTH ELECTRONIC AND HOT METAL COMPOSITION ARE INCLUDED.

AD Abbreviation for advertisement; referring usually to display advertisements. *See also* Add.

ADD Additional news matter; matter to be added to a news story. Frequently abbreviated to "ad."

AGATE Type 5½ points in depth. Agate lines are used to measure the length of newspaper columns and the depth of advertisements in hot metal composition.

ANGLE A division or phase of a news story.

ASSIGNMENT A reporter's allotted task.

BANK Part of a headline; a table on which type is kept after it has been set.

BANNER LINE A single-line headline in large type extending across page one.

BEAT A reporter's fixed post, such as the City Hall beat; a story printed exclusively by one newspaper.

BINDER LINE A single line of large type, used on an inside page, under which is printed an unusually long story or a series of stories referring to a general subject.

BODY TYPE The type in which most of the newspaper is set; generally 8 point.

BOX Type framed by rules to give a box effect so that the type is more prominently displayed.

BREAK The point at which a story turns from the first page to an inside page, or from one column to another.

BULLDOG An early edition.

BULLETIN Last-minute important news.

BUREAU A subsidiary news-gathering organization set up in an important center, such as Washington.

BYLINE The reporter's signature preceding a story.

CANNED COPY Written information sent to the newspaper by the publicity bureaus of organizations, or by press agents.

CAPS Abbreviation for capitals.

CAPTION The explanatory lines above or below a newspaper photograph, illustration or diagram.

CATHODE RAY TUBE (CRT) The television display screen in a computer terminal.

C.G.O. Means "Can go over" and designates stories of a character that permits them to be used at any time.

CHASE The metal frame in which the newspaper type is placed prior to the making of matrices and stereotype plates (hot metal).

CHECK UP To investigate; to ascertain the truth or falsity of information.

CITY ROOM The place where the news organization functions.

CLIPS Abbreviation for clippings; refers to the stories clipped from the newspaper and preserved, concerning persons and events.

COMPOSITOR The typesetter (hot metal).

COPY News manuscript; to make a copy of a story or headline in a computer directory.

COPY CUTTER The composing room employee who cuts the news manuscript into lengths or "takes" convenient for setting quickly and who has charge of the distribution of copy among the compositors (hot metal).

COPYREADER Same as copy editor; the editor who puts the copy in its final shape and who writes the headlines.

COVER To obtain the facts of a news story.

CRASH Failure of a computer system; problem that causes shutdown of editing and writing functions.

CREDIT LINE The line that designates, if necessary, the source of a story or cut. "By the Associated Press" preceding a story is a credit line.

CROSSLINE Part of a headline distinguished from the top and the banks.

CURSOR Spot of light on video display terminal screen that shows where keystroke will appear.

CUT Any newspaper photograph, illustration or diagram; also to reduce the length of a news story.

DATELINE The name of the city or town, with or without the date, which is placed at the beginning of stories not of local origin.

DAY SIDE   That part of the newspaper organization that functions in the daytime.

DEAD   News matter, particularly type, that has been eliminated and is no longer available for use.

DEADLINE   The minute at which an edition of the newspaper must go to press, or the time by which copy must be submitted.

DESK   The copy desk at which news copy is edited and headlined.

DIRECTORIES   Electronic file cabinets or storage units for edited or unedited material.

DISTRICT REPORTER   One assigned to a specified district.

DOPE STORY   A story, usually written under a byline, that describes a situation and gives opinions of others as well as of the writer concerning the situation. Many political stories are "dope" stories.

DUPE   Abbreviation for duplicate; if two stories giving the same facts inadvertently are printed in the same issue of the newspaper, one is a dupe. Dupe also designates the carbon copies of a story or electronic copy of a story.

EARS   Small boxes printed at each side of the title plate on page one; they usually contain the weather forecast, the newspaper's slogan, circulation figures or like information.

EDIT TRACE   Strike-through system of electronic editing that allows slot men to see changes made in original copy.

EM   A printer's measurement of type width.

EN   Half an em.

EXCLUSIVE   A story that is printed solely by one newspaper; a "beat" or a "scoop."

FEATURE   A story that is timely and interesting but is not, strictly, news. To feature is to display prominently.

FILE   To send a story by telegraph, cable, or portable VDT.

FILLER   Any matter that has no time restrictions and can be used when needed. Same as C.G.O.

FLAG   The title plate of the newspaper on the first page.

FLASH   A bulletin that gives the first brief information of an important event.

FLASHING   Alternate illumination and darkening of video display terminal screen, indicating malfunction or improper keyboarding.

FLIMSY   The carbon copies of news manuscript, which usually are tissue paper (hot metal process).

FLUSH   Even with the column margin on either left or right side; no indentation as for a paragraph. "Flush and indent" or "flush and hang" is a direction to set the first line of a piece of copy without indentation and to indent the succeeding lines at the left side. Same as hanging indentation.

FOLIO A page or a page number.

FOLLOW Sometimes used to designate a second-day news story; that is, a story developing from another the facts of which have been printed.

FOLLOW COPY Direction to the compositor to set the copy exactly as it is written.

FOLO Abbreviation for follow. A follow story also is one that is subsidiary, but related to another.

FONT A complete set of type of one size and style.

FORM A complete page of type.

FORMATS Computer codes used to determine type size, column width, and styling. To format is to put proper coding on a terminal story.

FUTURE A record of an event that is to take place.

GALLEY A metal tray to hold type (hot metal).

GEN To generate a story, or send it to the composing room for the production of a story as a slick-paper printout.

GENERAL ASSIGNMENT REPORTER A reporter available for general work, as distinguished from one who has a fixed post.

GOOD NIGHT The closing of the news department after the final edition; to "get good night" is to be released from duty.

HARD COPY Copy typewritten or printed out on paper, as opposed to video display.

HEAD Abbreviation for headline.

HOLD FOR RELEASE Designation placed on copy that is to be set, but is not to be used until the direction to do so is given by the editor in charge.

HOLDING Holding the paper is putting back the edition deadline to wait for an important news story.

HOT START System of restarting computer system after a crash or other temporary interruption.

HTK, HTC Abbreviation for "head to come"; the designation placed on the first page of a story rushed to the composing room in takes, to indicate that the headline will follow. Used only on hard copy.

INDENT *see* Flush

INSERT News matter to be incorporated in a story that has already been sent to the composing room and set in type. The copy of this matter is designated "insert."

JUMP The continuation of a page one story on an inside page.

JUMP HEAD The headline that identifies the continuation of a page one story.

KERNING Typographical process (in electronic editing) of tucking one letter under another, used for better appearance, and sometimes to make headlines fit.

KILL To eliminate from copy; to discard type as useless.

LABEL A headline that has no life or force, or a mere caption.

LATE WATCH After the rush of editing and printing the newspaper is over and most of the staff has gone off duty, a skeleton staff remains to handle late stories and late editions.

LAYOUT A sheet, ruled into columns, indicating where the stories or the stories and advertisements will be placed in the newspaper page.

LEAD Thin metal strips that are one, two and three points thick, used to space out lines of type. Also the process of spacing out (pronounced led).

LEAD or LEDE The introduction of a news story (pronounced leed).

LEG MAN A reporter who gathers facts but does not write them.

LOBSTER SHIFT Same as "late watch," or early watch on an afternoon paper.

MAKE OVER The process of rearranging a page, or a series of pages, to improve the appearance or to place new stories.

MAKEUP The process of placing news stories and advertisements in the newspaper page.

MASTHEAD The heading, often on the editorial page, that gives information about the newspaper.

MAT Abbreviation for matrix; the papier-mâché impression of a page of type from which a stereotype plate is made in hot metal composition.

METROPOLITAN EDITOR City editor.

MINION Seven-point type (hot metal).

MORGUE The place where newspaper clippings are filed.

MUST A designation placed on copy to indicate that it must be printed.

NIGHT SIDE That part of the newspaper staff that functions at night.

NONPAREIL Six-point type. It is also a unit of measurement for type widths, as the agate line is the measurement for depth.

OBIT Abbreviation for obituary; it means biographical material in general, not merely that of dead persons.

OP-ED The page opposite the editorial page.

PAGE DOWN "Page up" in reverse; to move a page down.

PAGE UP Moving material on the screen up by the same number of lines shown on the terminal at any one time. (On the Harris machine, there are 26 lines to a "page," the number of lines shown when the screen is full.)

PAPER A printout or "hard copy" of a computerized story.

PICA Twelve-point type.

PICKUP Type already set that is to be incorporated into new matter; also the direction to the composing room to incorporate such type with new material being set.

PIED Pied type is type that is disarranged or jumbled so that it cannot be used.

PLEASE USE Similar to "must," but indicates only that it is desirable to use the story so marked.

POINT A point is $\frac{1}{72}$ of an inch and is the unit of measurement for type sizes.

POSTSCRIPT A page made over between editions for imperative corrections or for important stories.

PRINTERS Composing-room employees who paste up pages under the direction of makeup editors.

PROOF An impression of type on paper, on which corrections and other alterations are made.

PROOFREADER A composing room employee who checks the proof against the copy to detect errors made in typesetting.

PUT TO BED Closing the pages for an edition.

Q & A MATTER Abbreviation for "question and answer" matter. Testimony frequently is printed verbatim.

QUERY A telegraphic summary of a story sent by a correspondent, stating the number of words available. The telegraph editor judges the story by the summary, and orders the number of words required.

RAILROAD The rush copy into type without close editing. This is resorted to only in emergencies.

RELEASE The order to print a story that has been set earlier and held to await instructions from an editor in charge. Also refers to "canned copy."

REPLATE Same as Postscript.

REPRINT Matter printed in late editions that has not reached readers of the early editions, and therefore is available for use in those editions in the following issue.

REWRITE To write for a second time to strengthen the story or to reduce it in length.

REWRITE MAN The reporter who takes the facts of stories over the telephone, assembles them and writes the story; he also revises copy written by other reporters to improve it or to cut it.

RIM   The desks at which the copy editors sit.

RULE   A printed line. The line between the columns of a newspaper is made by a column rule.

RUN IN   To incorporate into one paragraph a series of paragraphs or a list of names.

RUNNING STORY   A story that is sent to the composing room from the copy desk in a series of short sections; *also* a continuing news story.

RUSH   Designation placed on copy to insure speed in handling.

SACRED COW   Slang for a subject or story in which the publisher or higher editors are interested and which must be printed.

SCHEDULE   The city editor's record of assignments; the copy editor's record of the stories he has edited and headlined.

SCOOP   *See* Beat and Exclusive.

SCROLL UP, SCROLL DOWN   To move images up or down on the screen to follow a story, check on repetition, etc.

SEARCH AND REPLACE   Computer capability of individual machine programming to find a special word or combination of letters and substitute another word or combination of letters, all at the press of a button.

SECOND DAY   *See* Follow

SECOND FRONT   The first page of the second section of the newspaper; sometimes called the split page.

SEE COPY   Direction from the copy desk to the composing room to verify a part of a story by reference to the copy. "Out see copy" means that a line or lines have been dropped and the copy must be referred to so that they may be restored (hot metal).

SET AND HOLD   *See* Hold for Release.

SHEET   Slang for newspaper.

SHORTS   Minor, brief stories.

SKELETONIZE   The process of dropping words from cable copy so that the rates will be reduced. Skeletonizing employs some code words, but the main saving is on articles and other words that may be eliminated without causing confusion to the copy desk in the home office.

SLOT   Where the head of the copy desk sits.

SLUG   The word or words placed on copy to designate the story. Also a piece of type metal.

SPIKE   To spike is to discard copy, once by placing it on a spike.

SPLIT PAGE   Same as Second Front.

SPREAD A lead story and all its subsidiary stories constitute a spread; also a story that requires a "top head," that is, one that goes at the top of a column; also sometimes used to designate the head itself. This also applied to any story longer than a short.

STAR EDITION A one-star edition is the first; two-star the second; four or five-star is usually the final.

STET Let it stand; restore.

STICK The unit of measuring quantities of type. A stick is two inches of type (hot metal).

STONE The bench or table, whose top is stone or metal, on which the pages lie in the composing room while they are made up (hot metal).

SUBHEAD A line of prominent type in the body of a story to break up a long stretch of type and to indicate the subject matter of the type that appears under it.

SUMMARY A synopsis of a news story.

SYNDICATE An organization either connected with or separate from the newspaper that buys and sells news stories, features and other matter used by newspapers.

SYSTEM The overall computer system in use. At the *New York Times*, there are eight systems working off two computers.

TABLE General term for any tabulated matter.

TAKE A section of a running story.

TIP Information from within or without the newspaper organization concerning a news event.

TRANSFER To transfer a story or headline to another directory or system for storage, criticism or approval.

TRIM To reduce the length of a story; similar to Cut.

TURN RULE A rule has a broad edge and a fine edge. The ordinary position of the metal strip is with the fine edge up; but on the order "turn rule," the broad edge is turned up and is easily seen by the printer. It indicates to him that some correction or alteration is to be made at that place in the type (hot metal).

TYPO Abbreviation for typographical error.

VIDEO DISPLAY TERMINAL (VDT) The computer terminal, including television screen and keyboard.

WARM START Normal starting procedure for computer system at the start of a new workday or at the close of an old one. Directories are automatically purged of some entries during a warm start, according to overall computer programming.

WHEN ROOM Same as C.G.O.

INDEX